Soar Into the Skies of Hope

DAISAKU IKEDA

Illustrated by Alexandra Ball

TREASURE TOWER BOOKS

Published by Treasure Tower Books
The children's book division of the SGI-USA
606 Wilshire Blvd.
Santa Monica, CA 90401

All rights reserved.
Printed in Korea.

© 2016 Soka Gakkai

Illustrations by Alexandra Ball
Cover and interior design by Lightbourne, Inc.

ISBN: 978-1-935523-77-2

10 9 8 7 6 5 4 3 2 1

Library of Congress Cataloging-in-Publication Data

Names: Ikeda, Daisaku, author. | Ball, Alexandra, illustrator.
Title: Soar into the skies of hope / Daisaku Ikeda ; Illustrated by Alexandra Ball.
Description: Santa Monica, CA : Treasure Tower Books, [2015] | Audience: Ages 8–12- | Audience: Grades 4 to 6- | Includes bibliographical references.
Identifiers: LCCN 2015036231 | ISBN 9781935523772 (trade paper : alk. paper)
Subjects: LCSH: Buddhism--Juvenile literature. | Buddhist ethics--Juvenile literature. | Conduct of life--Juvenile literature.
Classification: LCC BQ4032 .I34 2015 | DDC 294.3--dc23
LC record available at http://lccn.loc.gov/2015036231

The citations most commonly used in this book have been abbreviated as follows:

- OTT, page number(s) refers to *The Record of the Orally Transmitted Teachings*, translated by Burton Watson (Tokyo: Soka Gakkai, 2004).
- WND, page number(s) refers to *The Writings of Nichiren Daishonin*, vol. 1 (WND-1) (Tokyo: Soka Gakkai, 1999) and vol. 2 (WND-2) (Tokyo: Soka Gakkai, 2006).

Contents

1 Let's Advance Together! 1

2 A Bright Start to the Day 9

3 The Power of Song 19

4 Summer of Challenge 29

5 Live With a Big Heart and a Big Smile! 37

6 Reading Is Fun 47

7 Let's Have Wonderful Encounters! 57

8 Time Is Precious 65

9 Greeting Others and Expressing Thanks 73

10 Being More Responsible 81

11 Be Unshakable Like Mount Fuji 91

12 A Lion Cub Is Never Defeated 101

13 Spreading the Spirit of Peace
 Throughout the World 111

14 The World Is Your Stage! 119

15 Opening Up New Possibilities
 Through Writing 129

16 Asking Questions Helps Us Grow 139

17 Inheriting the "Treasures of Life" 149

18 Shine as Bright Stars of Hope! 159

19 Build Great Castles of
 Happiness and Victory! 169

20 Shine as Suns of Peace 179

21 Making a Fresh Start Each Day 187

22 Spread Wide the Wings of Your Dreams! 195

23 Friendship Is a Precious Treasure 205

Notes 215

Soar Into the Skies of Hope

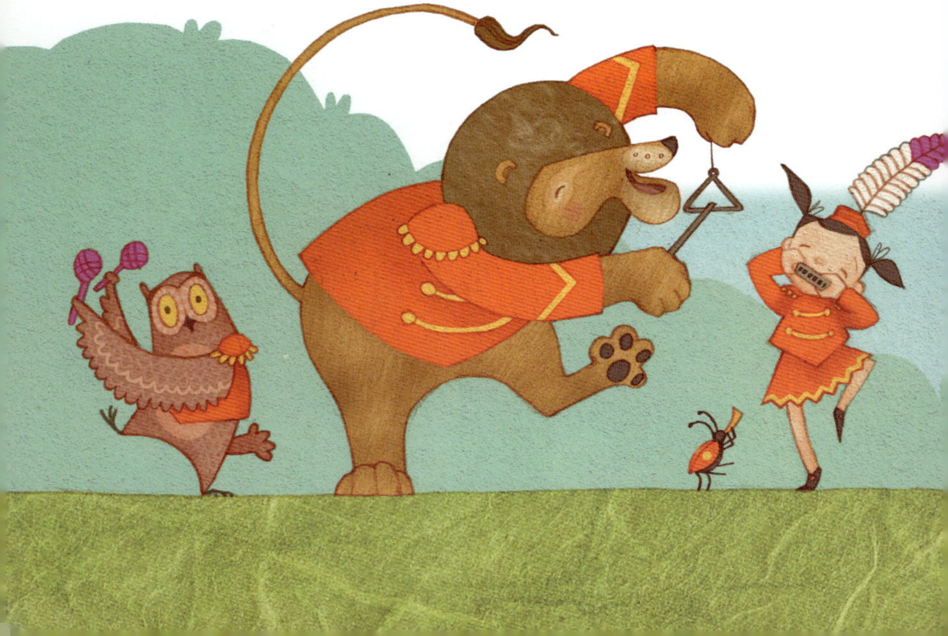

1

Let's Advance Together!

Do you know the origin of the Japanese word *sensei?* It means "teacher" or "mentor." The Chinese characters used to write *sensei* can literally mean "a person who was born before us." We also call those who teach us school lessons or important lessons about life, *sensei*.

I have had a lot of teachers whom I've learned a great deal from, starting with my favorite elementary school teacher. But out of all of them, the person I consider my greatest teacher in life is Mr. Josei Toda. He is my life's mentor and the second president of the Soka Gakkai. He taught me many things, and I am full of appreciation for him. Mr. Toda was fond of these words of the ancient Chinese thinker Confucius: "Respect the young."[1] It is impossible to tell how great a young person will become in the future, since everything depends on the efforts they make from now on. Therefore, youth should be treated with utmost respect. And just as he taught, Mr. Toda truly loved and respected young people.

Mr. Toda would often say to us, "As my successors, I hope you will surpass me." I now wish to say the same to all of you.

I am here to help you all become truly excellent people. I would do anything for your growth, as you are all so important and precious.

Let's begin our talk as if we are strolling together under clear blue skies in this sunny month of May, along a path where flowers are blooming, birds are singing, and butterflies are dancing in the air.

I am chanting that all of you can enjoy going to school in high spirits each day.

I went to elementary school during the dark times of World War II. The war continued for a long time. My four older brothers, who were in the prime of their youth, were drafted into the army one by one. When the war was finally over, we found out that my eldest brother had died in the conflict. I had loved and looked up to him very much. I will never forget how sad my mother was.

I am absolutely against war. I decided to devote my life to peace so that none of you, my beloved boys and girls, will ever have to experience the horrors of war.

Throughout much of my childhood, my father was sick and my family didn't have a lot of money. But my mother would always joke that we were like "grand champions" when it came to being poor. Her cheerful humor encouraged us.

I was physically weak when I was younger. But I used to drag myself out of bed early in the morning to go on my newspaper route and help with the family business of making edible seaweed. That period made me physically stronger so that later in life I could travel all around the world.

There were many difficult and sad times in my childhood. But looking back, I can see that even the times that I thought couldn't have been more terrible were crucial parts of my life story. I think to myself, "I'm so glad I challenged myself at that time."

Please remember that whatever troubles you may have in life, you can overcome anything.

I will never forget my elementary school friends, no matter how old I am. Over the years, I have bumped into some of them on the street and had happy reunions. A number of them later joined the Soka Gakkai with their families.

The school friends with whom you can be yourself and share unchanging friendships are lifelong treasures.

I also have many fond memories of times with my childhood friends. One freezing cold winter day some other boys and I lit the heater at school for a classmate who had a cold. But there was a rule that we weren't allowed to light the heater by ourselves without asking permission. All of a sudden, our teacher came into the room, and I was the only one he caught in the act.

"Go and stand in the hallway right now!" he said.

"Yes, sir," I replied.

I wasn't going to mention the other boys. But when they saw me about to leave the classroom, one by one they stood up to say that they were involved too. So we all lined up in the hallway. Even though we were scolded and made to stand outside the classroom, for some reason we couldn't help grinning at one another.

A little while later, the same teacher invited the group of us to his home. He welcomed us with a warm smile. We sat with him around his *kotatsu* (a low table with a built-in heater underneath) and listened to him talking about all kinds of things. We could then understand just how much he cared about us. He shared with us some words of Yoshida Shoin (1830–59), a samurai and educator whom he admired a lot. He made it easy for us to understand. The main point was that in order to become a great person, we should:

- **learn from a good teacher**
- **have a sense of appreciation**
- **and have good friends.**

That is exactly how I have lived my life, and I am still doing so now, seventy years later.

I believe in the power of friendship. I have spent my life making friends throughout the world for the sake of peace and to open a wonderful stage on which you can play an active role in the future.

Right now, there is nobody I want to talk with more than you, the boys and girls who are reading this book.

No matter what anyone tells you, the future belongs to you. In that sense, you already have within you the seeds of peace, culture, and education. Your presence itself is a source of hope for all.

You might sometimes be scolded by your parents. You might accidentally leave your homework or textbooks at home. You might hate studying or be bad at sports. But even so, in terms of the world's future, you are a bright sun of hope.

Nothing makes me happier than to begin a conversation with you through this book.

—*MAY 2012*

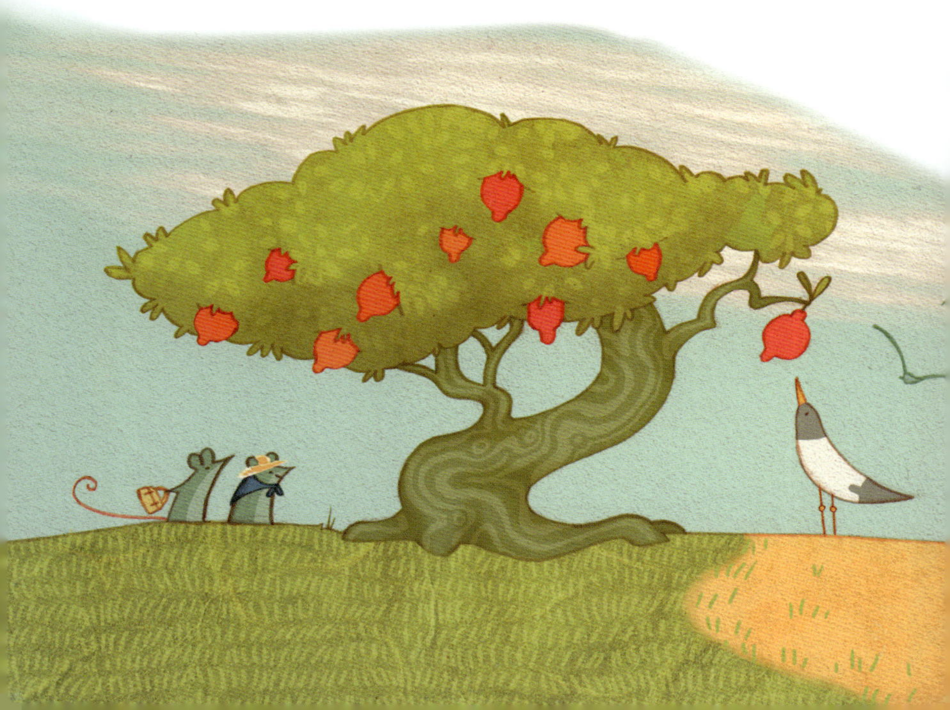

2

A Bright Start to the Day

What time did you wake up this morning? I am sure some of you got up really early! Even so, there are people out there who were awake earlier still. They had already started their day's work for the sake of all of us.

That is true of those who come to your house to deliver *Hope* [the Soka Gakkai's monthly newspaper for boys and girls]. Perhaps some of your parents also deliver the *Seikyo Shimbun* [the Soka Gakkai's daily newspaper]. On rainy mornings, it is particularly tough trying to carry so many newspapers and deliver them without getting any wet. It's easy to slip and fall too. Every day, I am chanting that our newspaper deliverers don't meet with any accidents. Let's be sure to show our heartfelt thanks to all those who, unseen by others, are delivering hope to our doors while most people are still sleeping.

There was a pomegranate tree in the garden of our family home when I was a young boy. The tree had a gnarled trunk. When the rainy season came, it produced striking red flowers and glossy, dark green leaves. In fall, we looked forward to eating its sweet-and-sour fruit.

I was often sick as a small child. And one time, I came down with a high fever and had to rest in bed. I had pneumonia—an infection of the lungs. I was delirious with fever. A doctor came to our house and gave me a shot to help me get better.

When I got better, my mother said to me: "Look at that pomegranate tree. Salty sea air and sandy soil are not supposed to be good for plants, but that pomegranate tree still bears fruit each year. Even though you're not so strong now, one day you'll definitely grow up to be big and strong too."

Our house at the time was less than ten minutes from the sea. But the pomegranate tree had managed to firmly root itself in the sandy soil.

The image of that sturdy tree is engraved in my memory, as is my mother's gentle voice. Since then, I have lived out my life with the vow to become stronger and to lead a healthy life so that I would not cause my mother to worry.

In my teens and early twenties, however, I suffered from a very serious illness called tuberculosis. At night, my temperature would go up and I had a terrible cough. Sometimes I even coughed up blood. The doctor told me that I would not live to see the age of thirty.

I then started to work for Mr. Toda. But after a while, his business faced hardships. I had to go without pay, and I couldn't even afford to buy warm clothes. I darned my own socks and wore summer clothes to work in the middle of winter. But my heart always blazed with hope and pride.

Later, after succeeding Mr. Toda as president of the Soka Gakkai (in 1960), I traveled all over Japan and the world to encourage members. I have also had chances to speak with presidents of countries and leading figures in various fields so I could open the path of peace and friendship for you, my young successors.

Nearly eighty years have passed since I made that vow before the pomegranate tree. I really did become strong and healthy, and I am still full of energy even now.

As I said earlier, it was during my elementary school days when I built the foundation to be able to work hard for kosen-rufu. I would wake up early to help out in the family business or do my paper route. Both are jobs that start very early in the morning. In winter, I had to begin work in the pitch-black pre-dawn hours.

My mother woke me every day. She'd say in a warm tone, "It's time to get up!" She later praised me for always getting out of bed right away. I was always good at getting up in the morning. "Why?" you might ask. I will teach you my secret. It's because I went to bed early the night before!

I know you might be thinking, "Is that *really* it?" But, in fact, it's often the most plain, normal, and simple things that are most important.

I woke up early and did my chores. Then I went to school where I studied hard and had a great time playing with my friends. After that I would read, because I loved books. At night, completely satisfied and worn out, I would become sleepy, go to bed early, and get a sound night's sleep. That's why I could spring out of bed when it was morning again.

"Early to bed and early to rise"—this rhythm has always been the source of my energy. I forged strong health by waking up early.

We all have the same twenty-four hours in a day. This is because twenty-four hours is the time it takes for the sun to rise in the morning, set at night, and rise again the next morning. In other words, it takes twenty-four hours for our Earth to rotate once on its axis.

Our daily lives, in rhythm with the sun, start in the morning and end in the evening. We have a clock inside that keeps us in time with the sun's daily movement across the sky.

Being bathed in the morning sunlight allows our internal body clock to run smoothly. Some recent studies show that if we wake up early and follow a regular rhythm, then our brain will also function better.

A bright start in the morning leads to a good day. If you continue in this way day after day, it will lead to a joyful year, a vibrant youth, and a well-lived life.

Winning in the morning when you are young is a source of lasting benefit.

My mentor, Josei Toda, also valued his mornings. In the early morning, when his mind was sharp and fresh, he would think very hard and come up with brilliant ideas. Those ideas led to the huge growth of the Soka Gakkai, which someone once described as a "miracle of the twentieth century."

Reciting the sutra and chanting Nam-myoho-renge-kyo each morning and evening also help us create a good daily rhythm for ourselves. They are the driving force for leading a healthy, happy life of triumph.

My greatest wish is that each one of you will always wear a bright smile and grow up in good health. Winning in the morning is crucial to this.

Please go to bed early, wake up early, and chant powerfully to get your day off to a good start. On mornings when you don't have much time, just chanting Nam-myoho-renge-kyo three times is enough. So long as you chant from your heart and with a nice, clear voice, it will reach the Gohonzon.

Of course, it is also important that you eat breakfast and train your body through sports or other activities.

Mongolian author Dojoogiin Tsedev, with whom I have spoken, writes in one of his short stories, "When you wake up early, you'll make new discoveries, and something will open up just for you, the discovery of which is sure to inspire you."[2]

With a smile and in high spirits, let's take another brave step forward today!

—JUNE 2012

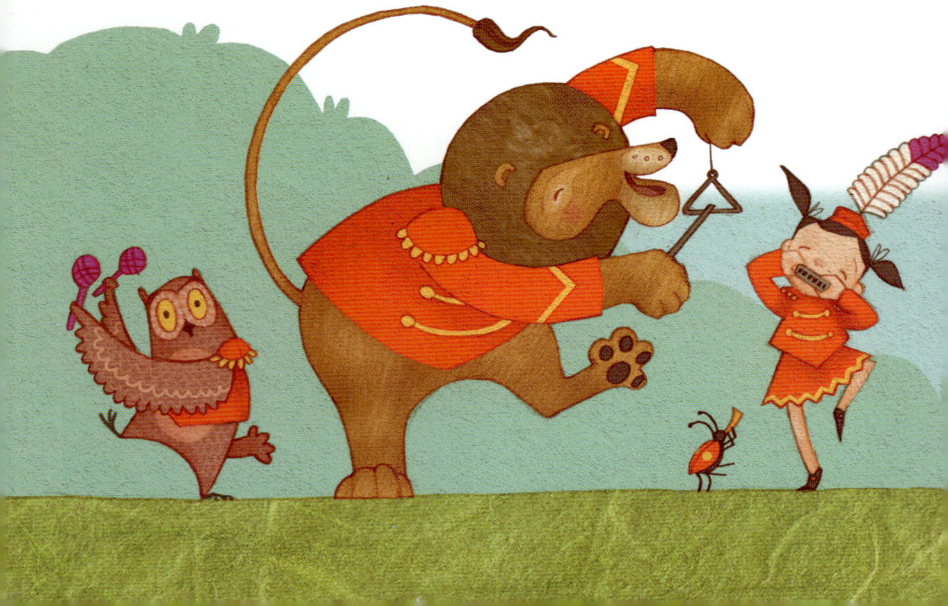

3

The Power of Song

Have you heard of a country called Armenia? I hope you'll take time to find it on a world map sometime. It is located where Asia and Europe meet. Its highlands take one's breath away. And its people shine with cheer and strength. They have won over a history of invasion, struggle, and hardship.

On June 15, 2012, some of my photos went on display in Armenia's capital. At the opening, a children's choir called the Little Singers of Armenia beautifully sang some songs from Japan. One of them was a folk song from Fukushima, which they sang to honor the people who survived the March 2011 earthquake and tsunami there.

I heard that their singing deeply moved the audience, who applauded with all their hearts. The choir later visited Japan and sang in sixteen cities [during July and August 2012].

Songs have a wondrous power that can rise above differences and bring people's hearts together.

I love songs. I have sung together with Soka Gakkai members many times, maybe even with some of your mothers and fathers. In the hope that it might bring them some joy, I have often played the piano or led members in song. And to encourage them in some small way, I also have written many songs.

I have a lot of CDs sent to me by the Soka schools choruses, the Soka University chorus, and Soka Gakkai chorus groups, also from the elementary school division. I listen to them every day.

When I picture you singing, it inspires me to take one more step forward and keep working hard for kosen-rufu.

Your lively voices fill me with energy. I'm sure all of you have your favorite songs. The elementary school division's song is "Be Brave! With a Lion's Heart!" It is really wonderful. In it, we find the lines:

Be brave!
Be unbeatable in spirit,
And set off toward a peaceful tomorrow. . . .

After the earthquake and tsunami, a large poster with this song's lyrics handwritten on it was found in one of our culture centers. It was untouched by the massive wave that hit. Since then, both children and adults have sung this song together. They encourage one another to be brave as they moved forward.

Whenever I hear the song, I feel that a new age is coming. I can just picture each one of you bravely making your way out into the world. It strengthens my belief that we will succeed in building a hope-filled future.

Why is it that the SGI has developed so greatly even though it faces many difficulties? One big reason is that no matter what we have faced, we have always held our heads high and sung together.

My mentor, Josei Toda, also loved songs. One of his favorites was called "Dainanko" (The Great Hero Kusunoki),[3] about a vow between a father and son. It opens with the famous lines:

Dusk falls on the lush greenery
of the village of Sakurai....

I once told Mr. Toda that we used to sing it in my elementary school. He seemed very pleased.

Whenever we, his disciples, passionately sang one particular line that talked about growing and developing quickly, Mr. Toda nodded deeply as if he truly understood our feelings as we sang.

We can tell others what's in our hearts through song. Even those things that can't be said well in words can be shared through song.

Songs can create solid life-to-life bonds. They lift our spirits and make us stronger.

Even when others have treated me badly, I have always sung songs. It instantly brightens my spirits and helps me to keep moving forward. This is exactly the meaning of "be brave!" We can "be unbeatable in spirit" through singing.

Some of you may think that you are tone-deaf and no good at singing for all kinds of reasons. Perhaps you can't reach very high or low notes. Or you can't find the right pitch or rhythm. You might not be able to sing as well as you'd like or memorize all the words. Or you might be too embarrassed to sing in front of others.

But don't worry and don't give up yet! No one can sing brilliantly from the start. I still get nervous when I sing in front of others.

But when we really try our best, our listeners will be touched. When we make a sincere effort, it speaks directly to our audience.

First, it is important to sing in a big, clear voice. Because if we can't be heard, we can't reach our listeners' hearts.

If you want to project a clear voice, you need to breathe from your stomach. Usually, when we breathe we use only our lungs, which are in our chest. But trained singers mainly use the muscles around their stomach, or their diaphragm.

When you can do this, you will find your breathing steadies. Your throat will relax, and the quality of your voice will improve. You'll find singing becomes more fun. It's also known that breathing from the diaphragm is good for our health. Singing in a strong, clear voice can actually improve our well-being in body and mind.

When we sing in a chorus, it is important to listen well to the music and the voices around us. Our ears are like windows to our heart. Therefore, it is important to keep our ears open.

Our determination to sing in unison as a chorus comes through in our voices, uniting our hearts as one.

Songs can reveal the singer's spirit and life condition. Therefore, we can learn a lot about the state of the world and the mood of the period from the kinds of songs that are being sung.

I am sure some of you belong to future division choirs. Thank you so much for all the effort you put into each practice and performance.

These were created based on my proposal. Since this was forty-six years ago (in 1966), perhaps some of your mothers and fathers were part of these groups too.

I sent a message when the groups were formed, saying: "I entrust to you Japan's future in the twenty-first century and the achievement of world peace. Please grow up into fine people."

Now I want to say the same thing to you. Your bright singing voices embody peace itself. They have the power to stop wars and are a source of hope for all people.

My good friends around the world have told me that upon their visits to Japan, the most moving thing was being warmly welcomed by the singing of our boys and girls.

Please remember in times of suffering or challenge that you always have the power of song. Then sing at the top of your lungs. Encourage yourself and all those around you. Cheerfully start over again.

I will continue to work hard to build a healthier and more peaceful world in which the boys and girls joyful voices resound.

Your singing voices always inspire me. I also take the future division chorus motto as my own—"Singing harmonies of hope for a victorious future!"

Today again, let's advance with energy, singing harmonies of hope.

—JULY 2012

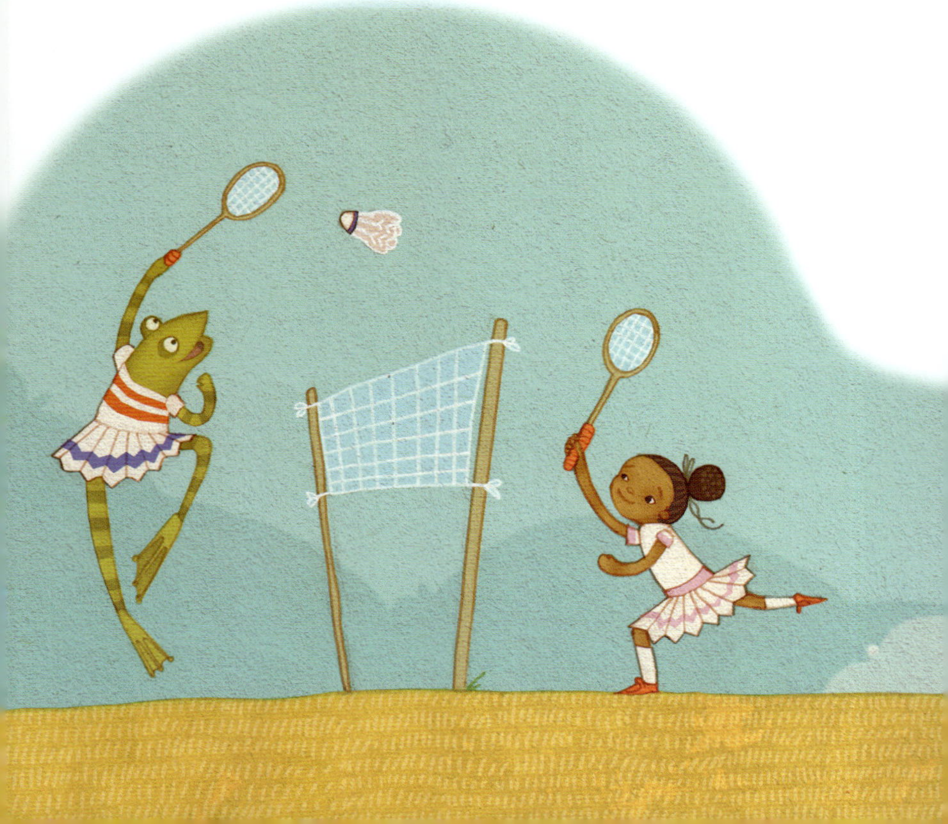

4

Summer of Challenge

This summer a Soka Family Gathering was held. The future division gave reports and gave a wonderful chorus performance. These inspired and delighted everyone, including parents and visiting SGI leaders from around the world. Thank you so much!

Your bright and lively growth in itself brings the greatest of joy to all our members. It is the ultimate hope for kosen-rufu.

In the Olympics in London [July to August 2012], some of my young friends competed. These are your big brothers and sisters who have graduated from the future division. They all made great efforts. I am sure that from among your ranks, too, will emerge future gold medalists!

I am chanting deeply and strongly with the firm belief that all of you will take your places on the world stage. You will shine as champions in all different fields.

Please have big dreams. And please study, play, and grow with lots of energy.

Today, I'd like to suggest a motto to make for a fun summer holiday.

That motto is: "Challenge!" That's right, challenge something. It doesn't matter what.

When do you feel like you're having the most fun? Of course, there are many ways to enjoy ourselves. But one way is when we set a goal and work our hardest to achieve it, even if it's difficult. Surely these are the times when we feel most alive and satisfied. This is true enjoyment.

Those who make it to the Olympics have to go through nonstop, tough training. But their sights are set on victory, and they know they are giving everything they can. So they feel very satisfied. Because they have this pride and joy, they can endure hard training.

Some of you, however, may have set yourself a target but couldn't stick to it for long. I understand this feeling well.

But even if you can stick to something only for a few days, that's fine. When you challenge something even for three days, you'll achieve three days' worth of growth. You should feel good about yourself for having stuck to it for three days. There's no need to feel bad about stopping after a few days. Just keep starting over. If you repeat this ten times, that makes a whole month!

Those who can renew their determination and try again are most admirable. They are winners. The important thing is to continue to challenge yourself and not give up.

Nelson Mandela (1918–2013), former president of South Africa and my respected friend, was truly a person of vast courage. He continued through all challenges. He was ten years older than me and fought to protect human rights until he passed away at age ninety-five.

He was a man whose resolve never wavered. He was in prison for more than twenty-seven years. That's ten thousand days. But he never stopped trying to achieve freedom and equality for all people. All this in a country where the black majority had been treated badly and discriminated against for so long.

Mr. Mandela cherished the poem titled "Invictus." *Invictus* is a Latin word meaning "unconquered" or "unbowed." Or more simply, the spirit to never give up.

In 1995, the year after Mr. Mandela became president, the Rugby World Cup was held in South Africa. South Africa's rugby team was inspired by Mr. Mandela. They burned with the spirit of *invictus*. They bravely overcame many obstacles. And they went on to win against teams said to be better than them, finally taking the cup.

The players were very happy to win for President Mandela and for all the South African people, through their invincible spirit.

Those who continue to challenge themselves in their own way, even if they lose sometimes, will certainly finish as champions.

Many years ago, I went to watch the sports festival at Kansai Soka High School. There was one student who became sick as he was running. He fell far behind the other runners in the long-distance race. Although he ran slowly, he did not stop. He was greeted with a big round of applause at the finish line. I gave him the white award ribbon I had been wearing as though it were a gold medal. And I praised his great efforts.

That student, who showed what it means to never give up, challenged himself in his studies too. Now he is a lawyer devoting himself to help ordinary people.

Whether you are studying or reading, having the spirit to continue a little bit longer will benefit you in the future. When you feel like giving up, spur yourself to study just five more minutes or read just one more page.

Some recent scientific studies say that it's very good for our brains when we feel a sense of accomplishment after working hard to do something. So when we challenge something new, our brain will become even stronger and sharper.

I have continued to write the serialized novels *The Human Revolution* and *The New Human Revolution*. I want to leave behind the great history of my mentor and encourage my fellow members. I write one page after another, one installment after another. Now the number of installments of both series totals more than sixty-four hundred. And, I am determined to continue writing, the best I can, and pass the baton of Soka to you, my young friends.

Anyway, a truly enjoyable and fulfilling youth is one you create for yourself through your own spirit of challenge.

Try to do even better today than yesterday and better tomorrow than today. Such efforts each day lead to a truly great life.

Another summer of challenge is here. Let's chant Nam-myoho-renge-kyo, the power for taking on fresh challenges. Let's start something new!

Wherever you choose, in a place where you can shine, set a new personal best.

My beloved boys and girls, I am praying sincerely for your health and safety.

I look forward to talking with you again in the next chapter. I am confident that you will have grown wonderfully through your summer of challenge. Please stay well!

—AUGUST 2012

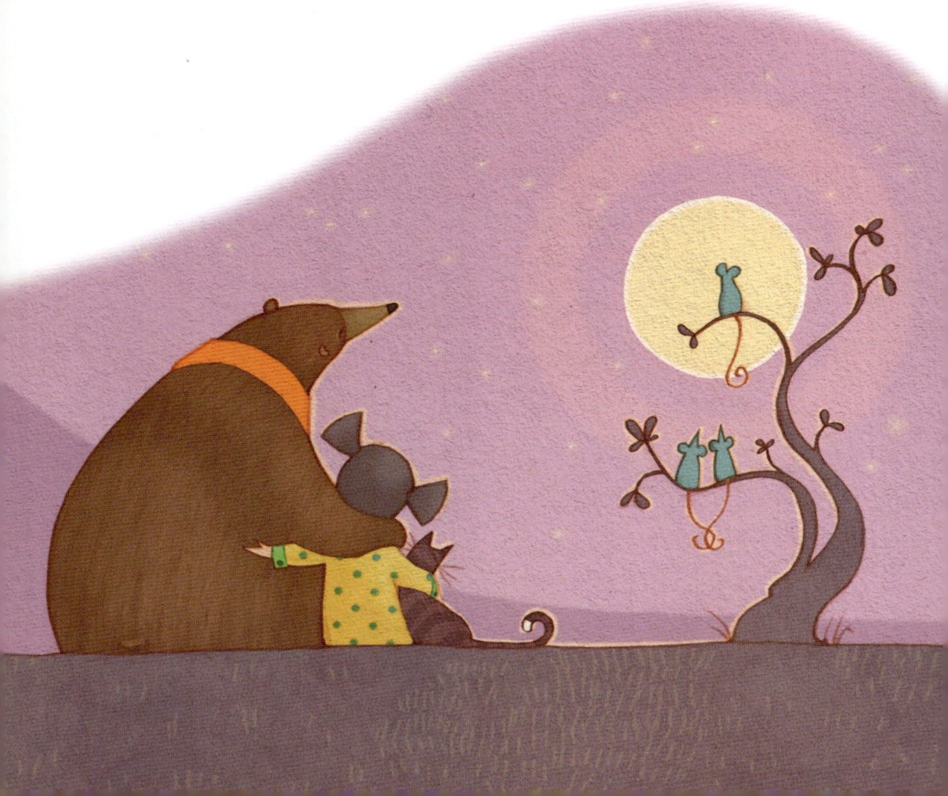

5

Live With a Big Heart and a Big Smile!

Today again, let's move forward in high spirits! Always moving forward is the spirit of true successors of the SGI. Just like the moon in the sky grows bigger each day until it's full, please grow bigger and stronger day by day.

Fall is a time when the moon shines with special brightness. The full moon that comes closest to the start of fall is called the harvest moon. Many think it is the most beautiful of the entire year. When I was young, we often organized moon-viewing parties to celebrate this annual event. We prepared rice dumplings and traditional decorations made from pampas grass. I remember how we couldn't wait to catch a glimpse of the full moon.

Moon-viewing parties have long been a custom in many Asian countries, including Japan. I also have many fond memories of viewing the moon with boys and girls and international students at the Soka schools.

When you look at the full moon, what patterns do you see? Japanese people see a rabbit pounding rice for rice cakes.

Gao Zhanxiang is a dear friend who is the chairman of the Chinese Culture Promotion Society. He told me that there's a Chinese tradition to pledge friendship and recite poems in the moonlight.

Do you know how far humans have traveled into space? As you may have guessed, it is the moon. The moon is roughly 236,000 miles from Earth. That's about the same as traveling around Earth ten times. On July 20, 1969, two American astronauts on Apollo 11 landed on the moon. It was the first time for humankind to land on another celestial body. Neil Armstrong (1930–2012) was the first man to walk on the moon. As he did so, he said to his colleagues watching over him from the space center on Earth: "That's one small step for man; one giant leap for mankind."[4]

From there, a new era of space exploration began. It paved the way for today's International Space Station and planetary research. When you are adults, there may come a time when you can travel into space, just like we can travel around the world today by airplane.

One person stepping on the moon's surface was a great step for humankind. But it was made possible by the unimaginable efforts of hundreds and thousands of scientists. And that's not including all their families and friends and others who supported them. If we included them, then it becomes tens of thousands, hundreds of thousands, and even millions of people.

The British historian Arnold J. Toynbee (1889–1975) once said that as impressive as the landing was the fact that so many people worked together to make it happen.

In fact, no progress has ever been achieved by one person's efforts alone.

I deeply respect you, boys and girls, because you are all precious messengers of the future. Each one of you has a noble mission for people's happiness and progress. Without you, the doors to a bright tomorrow cannot be opened. That is why you are so very important. Each one of you is a treasure the world absolutely needs.

Four years before the moon landing, in 1965, I established the boys and girls division with high hopes. Celebrations were held around Japan on September 23, the autumnal equinox. The eyes of the boys and girls shone with hope. They mirrored the bright future that lay ahead for kosen-rufu.

At the time, I gave the members five guidelines:

1) **Let's do gongyo and chant Nam-myoho-renge-kyo.**
2) **Let's study hard.**
3) **Let's go to school every day.**
4) **Let's not make our parents worry.**
5) **Let's be good and cheerful each day.**

Each year since, graduates of the division have grown steadily in the garden of Soka. They have soared into the skies of a hope-filled future.

I'm sure that some of your parents and grandparents are also graduates of the boys and girls division. They are all your seniors in faith who gently watch over you like the full moon.

If we open our hearts wide, then even the moon will become a bright and encouraging friend.

When I was a child, there were not too many street lights like there are today. I fondly remember reading books by the moonlight at

Morigasaki Beach near my home in Ota Ward, Tokyo.

The Brazilian astronomer Ronaldo Mourão once said, "The bright moon that illuminates the dark sky symbolizes the shining hope and dreams within each child's heart."[5]

I would like to share with you some lines from a poem I once wrote, titled "The Moon's Wish":

> *In the vast, serene sky,*
> *the full moon quietly appeared,*
> *encouraging all:*
> *"Have a big heart,*
> *have a big smile!"*

Nichiren Buddhism teaches that the heart and the treasures of the heart are most important. Let's live our lives with a big heart and a big smile that shines. It is the happiest way to live. The moon gently, brightly, and warmly reminds us of this.

Our hearts have no limits. They can grow ever bigger.

Nichiren writes, "The sun, moon, and myriad stars are found in one's life" (WND-1, 629). Within the heart of each one of you exist the sun, the moon, and the stars. By chanting Nam-myoho-renge-kyo, we can make them shine their brightest.

The March 2011 Tohoku earthquake and tsunami caused great destruction. And there's been torrential rains in Kyushu and other parts of Japan recently [in July and August 2012]. But the smiles of the boys and girls division members have been a huge source of hope for many people. People might feel as if they are in a dark tunnel with no end in sight. Even so, your shining lives have the power to brighten their hearts and revive their spirits like the light of the moon.

As long as you continue to study and grow, the SGI will be fine. As long as your brave singing can be heard, the future of kosen-rufu will be secure. None are more important than you, boys and girls.

Since the division's founding, it has been my vow and life's purpose to make the twenty-first century one of peace that echoes with your laughter. I have done my best to open new paths so that you can play an active role anywhere in the world.

Wherever you go in the world today, you will find SGI members living there. They are all waiting to see how wonderfully you grow up.

Please take a great step toward the future in your own way, with courage and a big heart.

I am always supporting you as I chant for your growth, good health, and victory.

—SEPTEMBER 2012

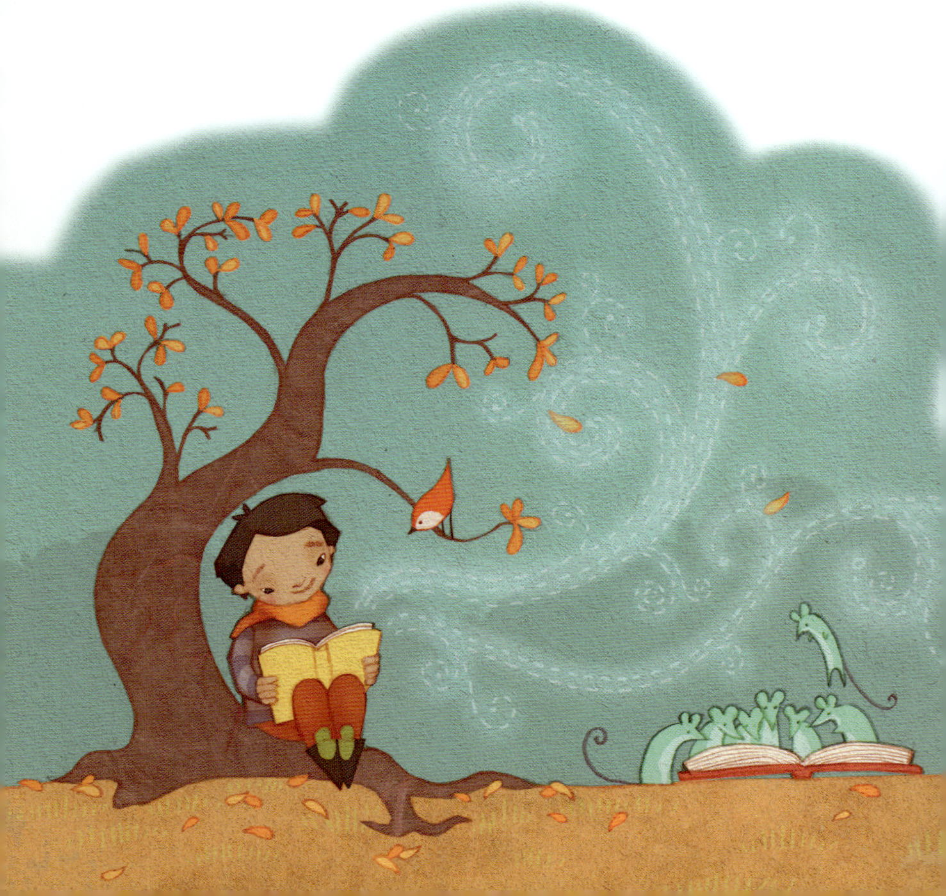

6

Reading Is Fun

Fall is a season of clear skies and bountiful treasures from the earth. It is a time of harvesting such important crops as rice, which farmers have lovingly grown to support our lives. In Japan, autumn is also considered to be a season when people, in accord with the great rhythm of nature, cultivate their bodies and minds. That is why we often call it the "autumn of sports" or "autumn of the arts." And because so many delicious foods are available in this season, it is also known as the "autumn of good appetite."

Today, I would like to encourage you all to make autumn a time to nourish your hearts and minds by reading good books. Some of you may think you are not good at reading. But please don't worry about that. If you can find even one book that you like, reading will become more fun. For centuries, people around the world have found great joy in reading.

In Japan each year, the two weeks from October 27 are devoted to the promotion of reading. I hope that you will all read good books and make this an enjoyable "autumn of reading."

Reading sets you on an exciting adventure. As a child, the German writer Herman Hesse (1877–1962) had an experience that taught him the pleasure of reading. In his home, there were bookcases packed with dusty old books that his grandfather had collected. The books all seemed a bit difficult, but two caught his attention. One was *Arabian Nights.* It contains such stories as "Ali Baba and the Forty Thieves." The other was *Robinson Crusoe.* This tells of the adventures of a young man shipwrecked on a desert island who overcomes various difficulties.

The young Hesse found the two novels interesting and exciting. He felt as though he had stumbled upon a wonderful treasure. From then on, he eagerly explored those shelves for more books to read. He later went on to write books of his own, which became famous throughout the world.

I would like all of you to start your own adventures in reading. Some books will practically invite you to read them. I hope you will take up their invitation and give them a chance. You will definitely make new discoveries if you do.

When I was young, I suffered from poor health and there were times when I had to be absent from school. But because I had books, which I considered friends, I felt a sense of freedom. Wherever you are, if you have books, you can travel to any age and any country. You can talk with great figures from history and the heroes and heroines of fantastic tales. You can experience the excitement of their lives and understand ten times, a hundred times over what it is to lead a great life.

Some of the most enjoyable moments of my youth were when I was reading. I hope that all of you, my dear friends, will experience this pleasure too.

Reading doesn't need to be difficult. If you start to read something and don't find it interesting, you don't have to read it to the end. You can go and find something more interesting or easier to read.

I'm sure that your leaders in the future division sometimes suggest good books to you. It's okay to put off reading those books for a later time. If you save the difficult ones for later and read something else in the meantime, you may find that the challenging ones become easier to understand when you get to them.

If you are a slow reader now, just keep on reading. As you go, you will get used to it and be able to read faster. If you are interested in a book one of your friends is reading, you could read it, too, and then discuss it with your friend later.

I hope you will also make use of your school and local libraries. You might, for example, borrow and read your way through the great works of literature. If you do, it will become an immense treasure for your life.

The German author Johann Wolfgang von Goethe (1749–1832) suggests making a habit of reading great works. Such a worthy habit, he says, can lift our spirits higher on sunny days and refresh our hearts on cloudy days.[6]

If all of you, at the age you are now, make a habit of reading, it will become an invaluable source of strength, wisdom, and joy throughout your lives.

In the natural world, autumn is a season when many living beings prepare for the harsh winter ahead. It is a time when their appetite increases, so that they can give their bodies the nourishment they need to survive the trials of winter.

An autumn of reading means the same for you. It is a chance to develop your courage and polish your wisdom. Then you can boldly face and overcome any challenge that the winters of life may bring.

One of the people I most admire is the great scientist Dr. Joseph Rotblat (1908–2005). He was a Noble Peace Prize winner and former president of the Pugwash Conferences on Science and World Affairs. He was a man of conviction, a man of peace. He devoted his life to trying to rid our planet of nuclear weapons, until he passed away at age ninety-six.

As a child during World War I, Dr. Rotblat was very poor and had only two small pieces of bread to eat each day. During such hardship, reading kept him going. He was inspired by the works of the French author Jules Verne (1828–1905), whose science fiction tales predicted a future of space and deep-sea travel. Such reading led him to think that the power of science could be used for the good of humanity and the world.[7] He came to have big dreams and studied very hard to realize them.

In our dialogue, Dr. Rotblat and I spoke of our wish that you, the young future leaders of the SGI, will inherit the dream of realizing peace and eliminating nuclear weapons from the face of the earth.

When I was young, I viewed reading as a way of training myself. My mentor in life, Josei Toda, would ask me almost daily what I was reading. He'd question me on what the book was about. No matter how busy I was, I eagerly read good books one after another. Thanks to the training I received from Mr. Toda, I became able to speak freely with world leaders on any topic of interest.

The term *gakkai* of Soka Gakkai means a "study association or society." Our organization is truly a place for learning. We have built it by continuing to develop ourselves through reading good books, learning together, and making new friends.

I hope all of you will challenge yourselves in reading as well. It will give you dreams to strive for and tools to realize them. It will help you show gratitude to your parents. It will help you contribute to removing misery and sadness from the world.

Reading is a steppingstone to your dreams. It is a bridge to friendship and a treasure that shines with eternal brilliance. The reading you do today can contribute to your own happiness, to the happiness of others, to the welfare of society, and to changing the world.

I wish one day that I might have the chance to meet you, and ask you about what you are reading.

—*OCTOBER 2012*

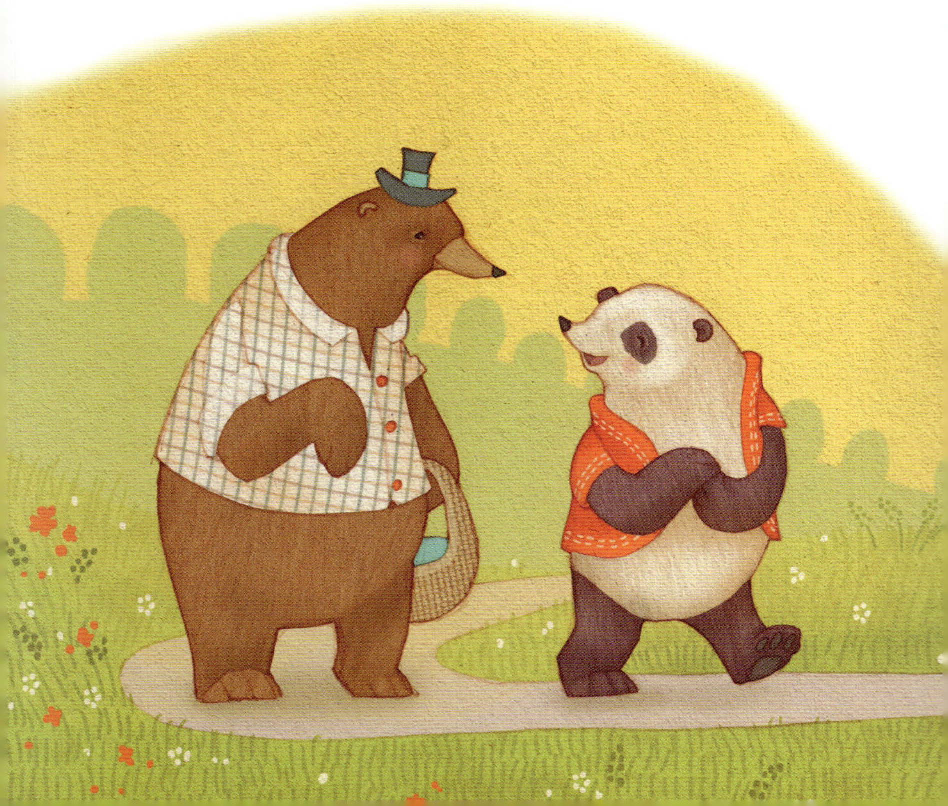

7

Let's Have Wonderful Encounters!

Have you met any new people lately? You probably get to meet new people at school events or on family outings.

A well-known proverb says: "The mountains do not meet, but people do." As human beings, we can go to new places and talk with others. We can become good friends and learn from one another. When we work with others, we can achieve amazing things. It is also a great source of joy, unlike any other.

I have met with people throughout Japan and the world. Just the other day (on September 11, 2012), I had a wonderful encounter with a group of SGI youth leaders from ten countries in Africa. They had made the long journey to Japan to attend an SGI youth training course. Each of them was a fine, brave person. They had all stood up to work for peace and development in their countries.

The members in Africa speak many languages. But all of them share the same mottoes of unity and victory.

Two days after my meeting with them, I greeted a group of sixth graders from Kansai Soka Elementary School, who were visiting

Tokyo. They brimmed with energy. Their faces were bright, their eyes shining with hope. I was delighted to see them. I felt that they would all go on to achieve great things in the future.

I actually wish I could shake hands with every one of you, boys and girls around the world. But even if we cannot meet in person, we can meet heart to heart.

Nothing can compare to diamonds in brilliance and strength. How are diamonds polished? By other diamonds. In much the same way, people are polished by other people. When we connect with good people, our lives will begin to sparkle like diamonds. They will radiate the light of good. Meeting with good people helps us grow. On the other hand, if we listen to bad people, we will stop growing.

Nichiren writes that if we mix with bad people, then we will follow what they say two or three out of ten times. In the end, we will become just like them (see WND-1, 310). I hope you never allow your pure lives to be muddied by such people.

Nichiren also urges those who really want to know about Buddhism to gather together and listen to the teachings (see WND-1, 206). In this way, he says how important it is to learn and study together. This is also the purpose of SGI meetings.

In fact, my own children learned about faith by attending Soka Gakkai activities. They grew by meeting with fellow members of all ages. There were times, of course, when they didn't want to go to a meeting. But my wife would tell them: "Even if you don't feel like going, afterward you will feel refreshed and energized. You'll be glad you went."

My wife also began attending Soka Gakkai meetings when she was in elementary school. One time Tsunesaburo Makiguchi, the first Soka Gakkai president, came to lead a discussion meeting at her home. She met him at the train station and guided him to the house. From a young age, she was aware how wonderful SGI meetings are.

At SGI meetings, we can hear others' experiences in faith. Members share how they won over their problems through Buddhist practice. People are making efforts to move forward in their lives. They are chanting Nam-myoho-renge-kyo and refuse to be defeated by obstacles. When someone is struggling, we warmly support and encourage them like family. We let them know we are there for them and chanting for their happiness. These gatherings of good, sincere people are truly unique in the world.

Dr. Vincent Harding (1931–2014), a well-known American historian, once went to an SGI discussion meeting. He was very impressed by how caring and helpful everyone was. He said that when a group seeks to change a hard situation, they need to keep encouraging one another that they can definitely succeed. One good way of doing this, he added, is by sharing and listening to one another's experiences.[8]

At SGI meetings, we meet with our fellow members and share our experiences. This gives everyone hope and courage. That's why these meetings brighten people's hearts.

Since the days of the first and second presidents, the Soka Gakkai has steadily held such hope-filled meetings.

Records show that over a two-year period during the harsh times of World War II, Mr. Makiguchi led more than 240 discussion meetings.

It was also at a discussion meeting (in August 1947) that I first met my mentor, Mr. Toda. I was looking for someone who could teach me about the correct way to live. At the meeting, Mr. Toda spoke about some Buddhist teachings, which I found hard to understand. But afterward he sincerely answered my questions. I knew I could trust him. I decided to follow him as my mentor and work alongside him in the great movement for kosen-rufu to realize peace and happiness for all people.

The SGI has now spread to 192 countries and territories. Today, every hour of every day, there is an energetic discussion meeting taking place somewhere around the world.

I have received many reports of how active you, boys and girls division members, are at discussion meetings. I hope you have noticed how happy it makes everyone to have you there. How much they applaud you. How much they appreciate what you do. That's because all of you are hope itself. Just meeting you, seeing you, and hearing your voices fill everyone with hope.

Those who leave SGI meetings filled with hope take those feelings home. When one family brims with hope, that hope will spread—to neighbors, to society, and eventually, to the whole world.

When people everywhere lead their lives with hope, they will be undefeated by sadness. And they can then live together in happiness and peace.

All of you have a life of great mission ahead of you. Therefore, I hope you will meet with as many good people as possible. Such encounters will brighten not only your own lives but also the future of the world.

—NOVEMBER 2012

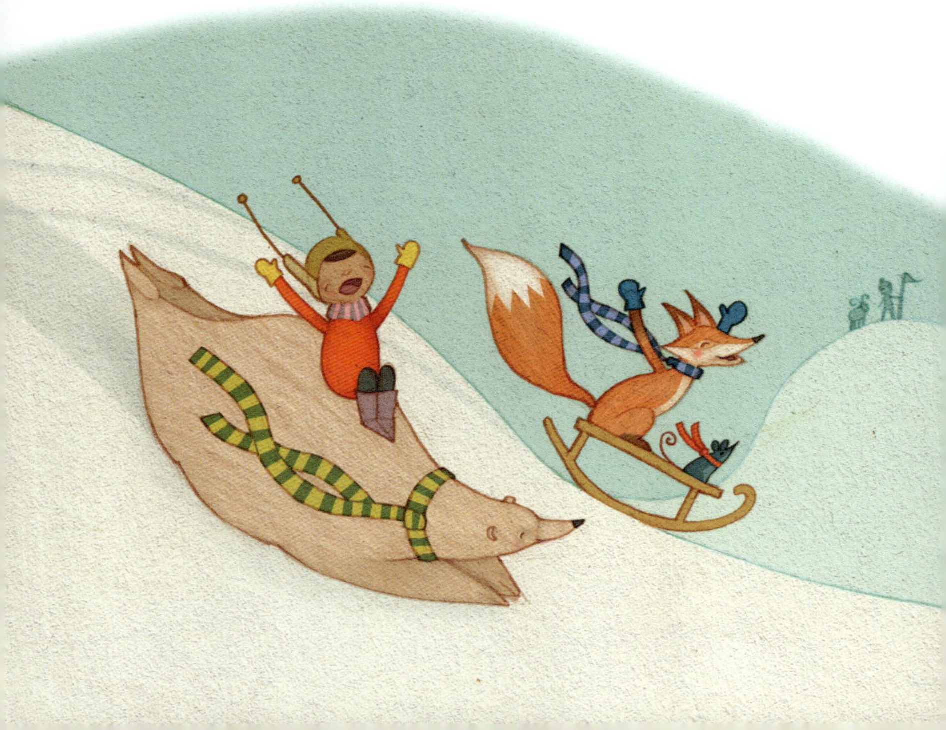

8

Time Is Precious

Fall, in which trees are dyed red and yellow, has ended. Winter has arrived.

I'm sure many of you made new friends this year and have fun memories. Some of you may also have some not so good memories, such as arguments with friends or not doing well in certain subjects.

But no matter what the past year was like, there is no need to worry. Remember the saying "All's well that ends well." This means that as long as you end the year on a positive note, you will make it a good one. And you will be able to start the new year filled with hope. So no matter what's happened up to now, the important thing is to look ahead and decide to do your best from now on.

Everything starts from now, from this moment, from today. If you keep moving forward cheerfully and steadily, you can learn even from your mistakes and do better next time. By doing your best now, you can make the most of what happened in the past. And you can open the door to infinite possibilities. What matters is that you think about what needs to be done now and then give your all to doing it.

I'm sure that some of you have heard or read the Buddhist story of the cold-suffering bird. It lived in the Snow Mountains in ancient India. The story goes that the nights in the Snow Mountains were terribly cold. Every night the bird complained that it was freezing to death and vowed to build a nest in the morning. But when the sun came out, the bird warmed up and began to play instead of doing what it needed to do. So when evening came, it complained again about the bitter cold. The bird continued in this way, freezing at night and playing during the day, and its whole life passed by without it ever building a nest.

For some reason, time flies when we're having fun but seems to drag by when we're having a hard time. Have you ever not done something you should have done and then got into trouble? I once didn't do my homework for an arts and crafts class. I still remember well how much grief it caused me.

Everyone has something they aren't good at or times when they just don't want to do what needs to be done. It may seem easier to put off the things we aren't good at or that we don't want to do. But the reality is that the more we delay, the more those things weigh on us and the harder they become. Like the bird that enjoyed the sunshine when it should have been building a nest, putting off what we need to do only causes us to suffer later.

If you study and do your homework when you're supposed to, then you can use the rest of your time to do the things you enjoy. That is much more productive. You also need time to play and rest. So use your days wisely. Set aside time to study, read, play, relax, and so on. When you make good use of your time like this, you can add many more enjoyable and satisfying hours to your day.

Some of you, though, may give up on doing something before you even try because you feel you wouldn't be good at it anyway. If you have this problem, I'd like to suggest a good way to overcome it.

Start by writing down your dreams or goals on a piece of paper. There's something really magical about the written word. Writing down what you want to do will put you on the path to get there. By the way, scientists have recently found that writing your goals down on paper stimulates the brain and makes you want to try to achieve those goals.

After writing down your goals, chant about them. Nichiren says, "Nam-myoho-renge-kyo is like the roar of a lion" (WND-1, 412). Like the roar of a lion, the king of beasts, Nam-myoho-renge-kyo is the greatest source of strength. Nothing can defeat it. When you chant, the lion-like courage and determination to realize your goals and dreams will well up inside you. The next step is to take action.

Here, you might find it helpful to make a "Victory Notebook." It's not that hard. Simply start by writing down all the things you want to do today and all the things you have to do today. Then decide on the order and time when you will do them. You can look at the notebook throughout the day to keep you on track and check off the items you complete. You can do this each day. If you have trouble figuring out how to do it, maybe you could ask your parents or one of your future division leaders to help you. Eventually, you'll get the hang of it.

In the SGI, we have the winning rhythm of setting goals, chanting about them, and taking action to realize them. Many of your parents and fellow members have followed this formula to challenge and achieve their goals. I hope all of you will make "Decide, chant, act!" one of your mottoes, and win every day.

Everyone has the same twenty-four hours in a day. But if you use those hours wisely, you can accomplish a week's worth of effort in a day. Or ten years' worth in a year. I have lived my life with that spirit. I treasured each moment and tried to learn, work, and strive as hard as I possibly could.

Nichiren writes that one day of life is more valuable than all the treasures of the universe (see WND-1, 955).

Time equals life. It is a priceless treasure. Those who value time, value life. Those who value life are the ones who will create peace in the world. The Japanese word for "mission" is *shimei*. *Shi* means "to use" and *mei* means "life." The important question, then, is, for whom and what purpose do we use our lives?

I have used my life to work with all my heart for the happiness of my fellow SGI members and the cause of world peace. My wish is that all of you will put your time to good use and grow into fine young people. I hope that each year you will feel proud that you did your very best. I also hope that someday you will come to use your precious time to contribute to the well-being of your parents and to the happiness and peace of people everywhere.

I am determined to use all of my remaining time in this world to work for the benefit of all of you, who are the heirs to the future. I will spare no effort for your sake.

My wife and I are praying sincerely for the health and well-being of all of you, our precious boys and girls division members.

—DECEMBER 2012

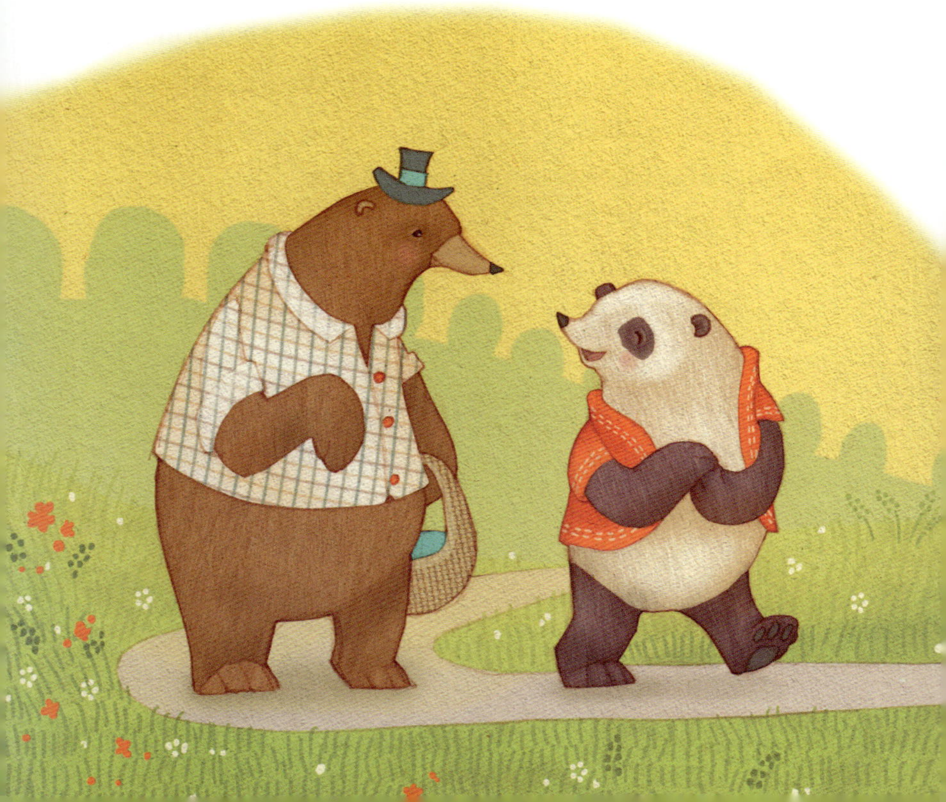

9

Greeting Others and Expressing Thanks

A new year has started. Did you wish your parents, relatives, neighbors, and friends a happy New Year?

My mentor, Josei Toda, taught me over and over how important it was to warmly greet others. In addition to scholarly subjects, he also taught me basic manners.

The way we greet others shows what is in our heart. It conveys our goodwill.

The lessons I learned from Mr. Toda helped me a lot when it came to making friends with world leaders. All of the truly great people I have met had a wonderful way of greeting others.

Whether I am meeting with the president of a country or with a small child, I try to greet everyone with utmost sincerity. That's because I respect each person's precious life.

Nichiren says that the Buddha appeared in the world to set an example of how human beings should behave (see WND-1, 852).

The way we greet others, therefore, is very important. I think that those who can always greet others in a cheerful, friendly way are truly admirable.

I remember that at the start of one year, someone said to President Toda: "Happy New Year! May this year be as good as the last."

"The same as last year won't do," Mr. Toda told them. "That means that we won't grow any more than we did last year. We need to be determined to make this year the best one yet."

The New Year is the perfect time to break out of our shells and make a fresh start. I have three suggestions for you.

The first is to say a cheerful "Good morning!" to everyone.

When I was a boy delivering newspapers, I used to always greet those I met on the street with an energetic "Good morning!" When you greet others brightly, it wakes you up and fills you with courage to take on the day.

When you get up each day, try greeting your parents with a hearty "Good morning!" At first, you might feel a little embarrassed. Your parents might even be surprised! But please give it a try. Your bright greeting will help start off your family's day on a positive note. This is also a great way to show your appreciation to your parents.

At school, too, make sure to greet your teachers, the staff, and your friends when you see them in the morning. It is important to look the other person in the eye and speak clearly. If you look away or mumble, it won't be much of a greeting!

I hope you will say hello to people not just in the morning but any time you meet them during the day. Greetings let others know that you care about them. In short, your brief greetings arise from your concern for others. Those who greet others are kind.

My second suggestion is to always be grateful for the food you eat. This includes appreciating those who prepare your meals. It also means feeling thankful for your parents and many others who work hard to take care of you and see to it that you have something to eat each day.

All of the food that we eat comes from living things—whether it is rice, bread, fish, meat, or vegetables. We eat plants and animals to get nutrients, energy, and strength. In other words, our lives are supported by many other living things. That is the reality of life. Therefore, being thankful for our food is to be thankful for the many lives that help nurture our life.

I heard about a boy who won a prize in an essay contest with an essay on this very topic. He wrote about coming to realize that he should be deeply thankful for the plants and animals whose lives help support his. He also came to understand that wasting food meant wasting those lives.

I feel the same way. We should never take our food for granted. Many children in the world suffer because they don't have enough to eat.

Eating keeps us alive. I hope you will also be thankful for the farmers and fishers and all of their hard work. Please eat your fill and grow up to be strong and healthy.

My third suggestion is to thank others for their kindness. I'm sure that you often thank others and that others also thank you. How do you feel when someone thanks you? I'm sure all of you feel quite happy.

Thank you is a magic phrase that brings joy to both the person who says it and the person who hears it. Those who feel and express appreciation have beautiful hearts. Those who can appreciate others' kindness will grow into leaders who can work for the happiness of others.

Nichiren constantly thanked his followers. He never failed to thank them for their sincerity, sending them letters upon letters of encouragement.

I, too, am always thanking my friends around the globe for their support and friendship.

"Thank you" in Japanese is *arigato;* in Chinese, *xie xie;* in Korean, *kamsahamnida;* in Spanish, *gracias;* in French, *merci;* in Russian, *spasibo;* in Swahili (which is spoken in many countries of Africa), *asante;* and the list goes on and on.

I will say "thank you" again today, cherishing the belief and wish that when we all show more gratitude for one another, the world will become a happier and more peaceful place.

Sometimes it takes courage to greet another person. Even if someone seems unfriendly, it's important to remember that they are human beings just like you. When you bring forth the courage to cheerfully greet people, no matter what their mood, you can open the door to their hearts. Your words also have the power to bring joy to your friends who are struggling or feeling down.

Your energetic greetings can brighten your homes, classrooms, and neighborhoods.

I have made a fresh determination to work even harder to open the way to the future for all of you, my young friends.

Each morning, I greet you in my heart, imagining your cheerful greetings echoing out in return.

—JANUARY 2013

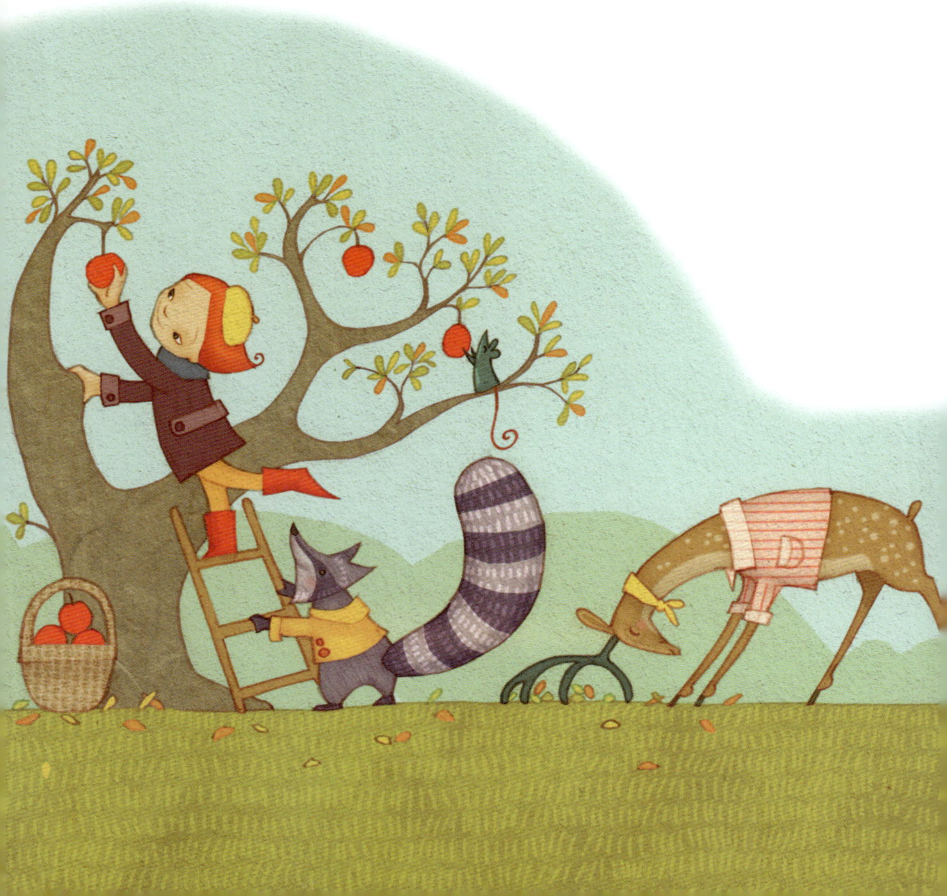

10

Being More Responsible

In the Soka Gakkai, February is special. This month we traditionally make extra efforts to share Nichiren Buddhism with others.

Cold as it is, I love February. That's because February 11 is my mentor's birthday. My wife and I celebrate this day each year.

One February in my youth (in 1952), filled with gratitude for my mentor, I did my best to introduce Nichiren's teachings to as many people as possible. And a record was set. That's how the SGI's "February Tradition" came into being. That is the pride of my youth.

Unbowed by the cold weather and in high spirits, please keep challenging yourselves in your studies, your reading, and your after-school activities.

Mr. Toda often used to say to young people: "I'm going to do kosen-rufu. Do you want to help me?" He never forced others to take part. He was resolved to achieve the goal of kosen-rufu on his own, if he had to. We, his disciples, joined him in his struggle and vowed to do anything we could to help him.

"I will take full responsibility!"—this is the spirit of a true leader of kosen-rufu.

From my mentor, I inherited a strong sense of responsibility. I feel this is a precious treasure. I stood up and resolved to devote my life to kosen-rufu—that is, to world peace and happiness for all people.

"I will do it, even if no one else does!" I hope that all of you, my young friends who will be wonderful leaders in the future, will develop such a sense of responsibility as well.

Doing so is not difficult. You can start with something simple, like tidying up your room. Some of you are probably thinking, "I'm hopeless at that!" But tidying up just means taking care of things yourself. If you can make this a habit, you will start to develop a sense of responsibility.

A German proverb says: "Order is half of life." That's how important it is to keep things tidy and in order.

What is the point of keeping things tidy? So you can find what you want when you want it. This applies to dishes and clothing too. If you don't put them back in their proper place when they're clean, you'll have to search for them the next time you want to use or wear them. Tidying up means putting things back where they belong.

Experts in the art of tidying up provide us with many helpful tips. Many advise to give set places, or "homes," for all of your things. A messy space comes about because you haven't given your things a home, and they get scattered everywhere. Once you decide where to put things, you can put labels on drawers, shelves, storage boxes, and the like to indicate what goes where. For instance, "school things," "sports equipment," "toys," "my treasures," and so forth. That will make it easier to find things when you need them.

For those of you who aren't very good at this, try setting aside a few minutes each day for cleaning time. If you do a little bit of cleaning up every day, instead of all at once, you'll find that it's not so hard to keep tidy. And your things will always be organized. You can also use this time to check that you have everything ready to take to school the next day.

Japanese schools have a set cleaning time, when students clean and tidy their classrooms. This helps the students develop a sense of appreciation for the school facilities and allows them to practice being neat.

The habit of tidying up I learned as a boy in school became very useful to me when I entered the workforce.

There is a Buddhist story that tells of a wealthy man called Sudatta. He built the famous Jetavana Monastery for his teacher, Shakyamuni Buddha, and his fellow Buddhists. It's a building that might be likened to our SGI centers today.

Sudatta gladly took on the tasks that others often disliked. So each morning he got up to sweep the monastery's grounds.

One day, Sudatta was called away suddenly and he couldn't do his regular cleaning. Shakyamuni, who had been watching his behind-the-scenes efforts, picked up a broom and started sweeping. Seeing Shakyamuni do so, other disciples quickly joined him.

When they were done cleaning, Shakyamuni said to his disciples: "Through cleaning, you also cleanse your heart. You can help purify the hearts of others too. And you will become more beautiful and increase your protection from the Buddhas and heavenly deities."

The next morning when Sudatta came to do his cleaning, Shakyamuni and a group of followers greeted him with a deep bow of respect. They wanted to deeply thank him for his noble daily efforts.

Cleaning and tidying up not only benefit your own life, but they can brighten the lives of your friends and families as well.

Recently, we had a big snowfall in Tokyo (January 2013). A group of dormitory students and baseball and soccer team members of the

Tokyo Soka Junior and Senior High Schools went out to shovel the snow. They cleared the road and sidewalk in front of the local railway station, which made the neighbors very happy.

Those who can keep their things organized also have organized minds. I believe it helps them do well in their studies too.

You'll also notice that books on library shelves are kept in their proper order. This way, everyone can quickly find the books they want to read.

Speaking of books, the Soka Gakkai's history began with a book that was the result of a lot of rearranging and organizing. As you may know, the Soka Gakkai's founding president, Tsunesaburo Makiguchi, was a principal at an elementary school. Whenever he had a spare moment, he would jot down his ideas about education on scraps of paper or the backs of old envelopes. Other people couldn't understand how important these notes were. But Mr. Toda did. And he organized them into the renowned book *The System of Value-Creating Education.*

Through Mr. Toda's skillful organization, a new theory of education came to light, presented in a way that was true to his mentor's spirit.

Being tidy can also help avoid accidents. In an earthquake, for example, items carelessly piled up on shelves can easily fall and cause injury if they land on someone's head.

Whenever I visit one of our centers, I make a point of doing a thorough safety check. I check that everything is kept tidy and in order, that doors and windows are locked properly, that there are no fire hazards, and so on.

Paying attention to small things is important. I feel very responsible to ensure the safety of our members.

Those who strive to realize a goal, no matter how small, whether others are aware of their efforts or not, are truly admirable.

Those who can take care of things themselves will surely become wonderful future leaders.

Those who try something and—even though they may not be good at first—keep at it until they succeed are real winners.

With our surroundings tidy and our minds refreshed, let's make this important month of February a bright and enjoyable one.

—*FEBRUARY 2013*

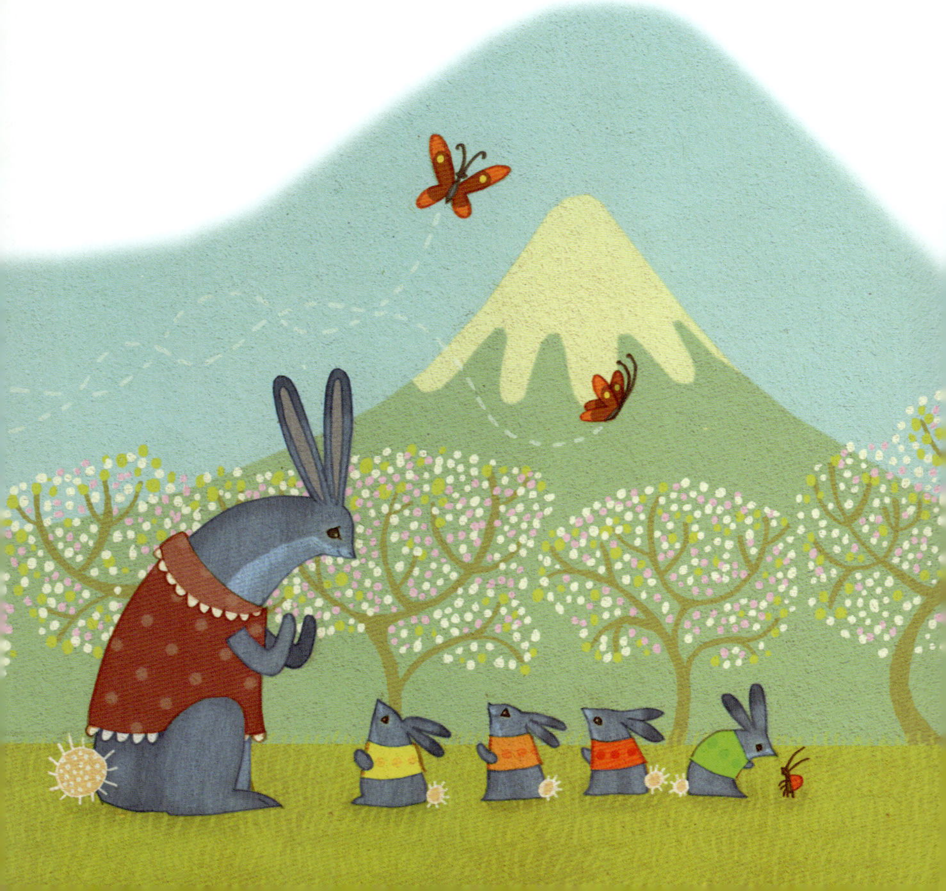

11

Be Unshakable Like Mount Fuji

As we enter March, the harsh winter cold is slowly letting up. Many animals are awakening from their deep sleep. Buds that were patiently waiting for warmer weather are beginning to blossom. It is the season when everything is coming to life.

The spring month of March is also a time of new departures.

My heartfelt congratulations to those who will graduate from elementary school! You have all worked very hard these past six years.[9] I would like to congratulate you, shaking hands with each one of you in my heart.

I especially want to applaud, with all my heart, the great efforts of those affected by the March 2011 Tohoku earthquake and tsunami. You have moved forward together in the face of every obstacle you've come across.

To all those going on to junior high school, please join me in continuing to walk the path of hope, even more brightly and positively.

Some of you will be moving up a grade in elementary school. Now is also a chance for each of you to make a fresh determination to work even harder in the new school year.

To make a determination is turning on the switch for growth. It is starting up the engine that will propel you forward.

When entrusting me with important goals, Mr. Toda would always ask me, "Can you do it?" And I would answer him resolutely, "Yes, I will!"

There were many times when everyone said it was impossible. But I had made a determination in front of my mentor and promised to achieve that goal. So I chanted earnestly and challenged myself to the fullest, believing I could surely achieve it. When I did this, more and more strength came forth. In this way, I overcame each hardship, never giving up. And each time, I grew stronger and was able to progress and improve myself. This is how I spent my youth.

It has now become a tradition for the graduations of the Soka elementary, junior high, and high schools in Japan to be held on March 16 each year.

On that date in 1958, youth division members, including me, gathered for a ceremony with President Toda. There we expressed our determination to carry on his spirit and continue striving for the sake of world peace and the happiness of all people. Six thousand youth from across Japan hurried to the foot of Mount Fuji that day. I, then thirty years old, was put in charge of ensuring the ceremony's complete success.

Mr. Toda, who had been seriously ill the previous year, was still very weak and having trouble even walking. Despite his condition, however, he arranged to have hot pork soup served to the youth who had traveled long distances to gather in the early morning chill. His sincere concern for us warmed our hearts.

At the ceremony, which I opened as emcee, Mr. Toda called out to the youth: "I leave the future to you. I'm counting on you to realize kosen-rufu!" And, he confidently declared: "The Soka Gakkai is the king of the religious world!"

Mount Fuji, the king of mountains in Japan, was watching over everything. As President Toda's disciples, we firmly resolved to follow in his footsteps and develop the strength of champions, unshakable like Mount Fuji. We vowed to advance kosen-rufu and form friendships with many people, including great world leaders. And today, as you can all see, the SGI has indeed grown into a global organization.

Mount Fuji's beauty is breathtaking. Soaring to a height of 12,388 feet, it is Japan's highest peak. That there are no other tall mountains nearby makes it all the more special.

Because it is such a high mountain, however, fierce winds often blow at the summit. Mount

Fuji is in constant battle. But without giving the slightest hint of this struggle, it stands firm throughout the four seasons, encouraging us silently.

I once wrote this poem:

A blizzard rages,
yet resolutely stands
Mount Fuji.

When I was in the fifth grade, my homeroom teacher, Mr. Kohei Hiyama, taught me something important through a scene from a book. The book is *Musashi* by Eiji Yoshikawa (1892–1962). The novel's hero is the master swordsman Miyamoto Musashi. He speaks to his young student as they look at Mount Fuji in the distance. "Instead of wanting to be like this or that, make yourself into a silent, immovable giant. That's what the mountain is."[10]

I felt as if my heart was suddenly filled with light. Since then, I have treasured this quote. It has become one of my favorites. I told myself: "No matter how tough it gets, I will be like Mount Fuji, never running away from difficulties!" In this spirit, even when I was ill, I was able to challenge myself to read and study. When my family was struggling, I supported them by delivering papers and helping out with our seaweed business.

During World War II, our house was burned down, my eldest brother was killed, and our family lost everything. After the war, I began working at President Toda's company. Even then there were many times I just wanted to give up. Each time, however, I reminded myself of Mount Fuji and did my best to rise above my problems. I continued to challenge the obstacles before me head-on. I was determined to let nothing defeat me and to show others what I could do. Through such efforts, I was able to actualize all of President Toda's dreams and goals.

I once shared this spirit of "being unshakable like Mount Fuji" with former Soviet president Mikhail Gorbachev. He's a dear friend who remains committed to world peace. I have heard that Mr. Gorbachev displays one of my photographs of Mount Fuji on the wall of his office and enjoys looking at it every day.

At the March 16 ceremony, I inherited the most important thing from President Toda: the baton of kosen-rufu, the noblest mission of realizing world peace.

In a relay race, when one runner passes the baton to the next, they both need to be running at full speed. In the same way, we as disciples should not simply wait for the baton to be placed in our hands. We need to make a determination and be running at full speed as we accept the baton from our mentor.

I am passing on the baton to all of you, my beloved friends of the boys and girls division, who are now running toward the future, full of hope.

March 16 will soon be here again. It will be a day to cheerfully celebrate our new departure.

All the pathways of friendship and peace I dedicated myself to opening throughout the world are there for each one of you.

Please advance with unshakable confidence like Mount Fuji!

Please win again today as champions!

To this end, I will continue to chant Nam-myoho-renge-kyo for you each day and to cheer you on.

Always unshakable,
Mount Fuji urges us
never to be defeated.

—MARCH 2013

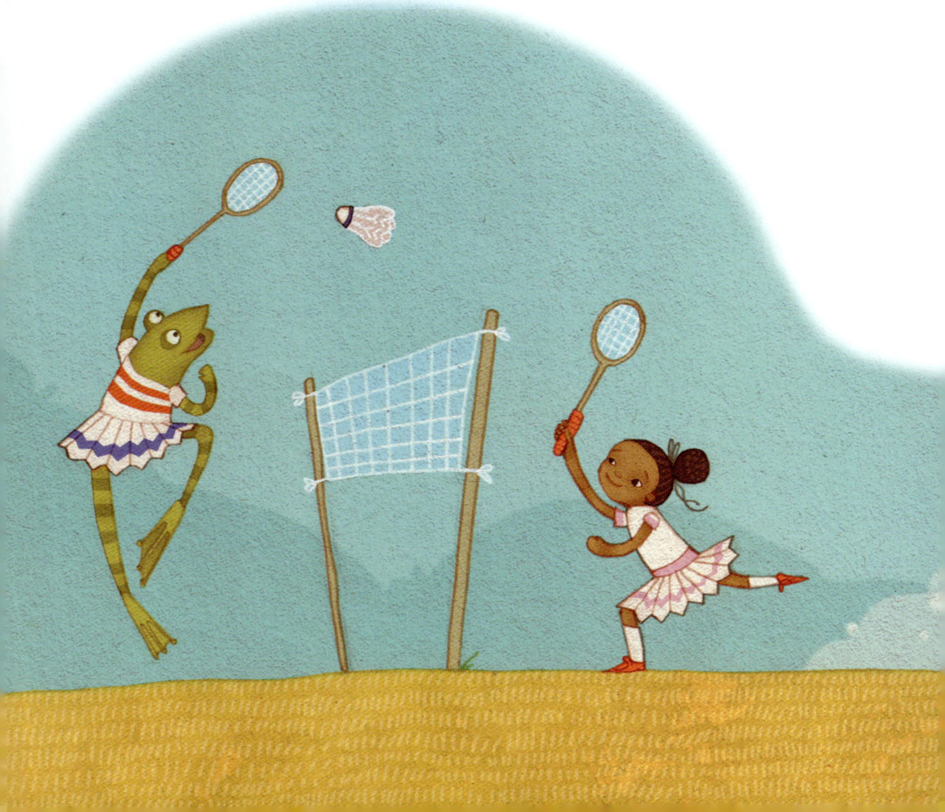

12

A Lion Cub Is Never Defeated

To those of you who have just entered elementary school, my heartfelt congratulations![11] I have been eagerly awaiting your entrance. I would also like to congratulate your entire family.

Congratulations as well to those of you who have moved up a grade!

Some of you may have also moved to a new school. With changes in your school or classroom environment, some of you may be afraid that you won't be able to make new friends.

But there is no need to feel worried. Please be assured that as you go about your day confidently and cheerfully, you will definitely be able to make wonderful friends.

As the saying goes: "Friendship doubles our joy and halves our sorrows."

Please treasure each new encounter and spread wide your wings of friendship in a way that is true to yourself!

Among my good friends was the late Dr. Linus Pauling (1901–94). He was a great chemist who was awarded the Nobel Prize in Chemistry and the Nobel Peace Prize. I once asked Dr. Pauling, also famous for his research on vitamin C, "Is there any medicine that could make us smarter?" Dr. Pauling responded with a smile, "The only way is effort and more effort." True to his own words, Dr. Pauling was a person who made great effort and had the spirit to never be defeated.

When Dr. Pauling was in the fourth grade, his home, which was also his father's drugstore, caught on fire and was damaged. To make matters worse, his father passed away due to illness the following year.

Despite his sorrow, Dr. Pauling worked part time and put his all into his studies, which enabled him to attend university.

Those who have had many hardships can better understand other people's struggles. The more difficulties you face, the more you can encourage your friends. So having problems and worries doesn't necessarily make you unhappy, but being defeated by them does.

Nichiren inscribed the Gohonzon and spread Nam-myoho-renge-kyo so people could overcome life's obstacles and achieve true happiness and help others do the same.

He called upon his disciples: "Each of you should summon up the courage of a lion king and never succumb to threats from anyone. The lion king fears no other beast, nor do its cubs" (WND-1, 997).

The lion is the king of the animal world. The lion king fears nothing, no matter how strong its opponent may be. No matter what happens, it advances fearlessly.

You each possess within you this unsurpassed courage of the lion king. Chanting Nam-myoho-renge-kyo enables you to tap this inner strength you possess.

Nam-myoho-renge-kyo could be said to be the name of this invincible heart of the lion king. When someone calls your name, you naturally respond, don't you? In the same way, when you chant Nam-myoho-renge-kyo, you are calling forth the heart of the lion king. You are able to bring forth courage, wisdom, the strength to live, and compassion to care for others. Therefore, those who chant can make their lives shine their strongest and brightest.

During World War II, President Makiguchi resisted the oppressive Japanese militarist authorities, and called out: "Stand up fearlessly and confidently like lion kings!"

After the war ended, my mentor, Josei Toda, as Mr. Makiguchi's disciple, brimmed with the courage of a lion king. And he resolved to eradicate misery from the earth.

I first met Mr. Toda when I was nineteen. Since then, I have earnestly chanted, overcome illness, and actualized all of Mr. Toda's plans and dreams.

A lion cub carries on the spirit of the lion king.

All of you who will shoulder the future are, without exception, lion cubs. A lion cub is strong. A lion cub is unafraid. A lion cub charges ahead at full speed. A lion cub roars out against injustice. A lion cub protects its friends. A lion cub is never defeated.

Even though you may not be good at studying now, or are physically weak, or are being bullied, or are having problems at home, nothing changes the fact that you are a lion cub. So don't let such things get you down! A lion cub will definitely grow to become a great lion.

There may be times when things don't turn out as you had hoped or you can't gather enough courage. Or maybe you feel as if your problems will get the better of you. In Buddhism, we compare a mind filled with such thoughts to a tarnished mirror. No matter how beautiful a mirror may be, if it remains tarnished, it won't reflect anything. But if you polish the mirror, it will begin to shine brilliantly like a jewel.

The same thing is true of your mind and spirit. Chanting Nam-myoho-renge-kyo is the best way to polish your mind and spirit, making everything clear. If you chant, your life will begin to shine. You will become more motivated and energized, and you'll become more bright and alert.

Through the efforts of the SGI, Nam-myoho-renge-kyo has now spread around the world. In those places, there are many boys and girls just like you who are also chanting.

Even though we may speak different languages—such as Japanese, English, Portuguese, Spanish, Korean, and so on—we all chant Nam-myoho-renge-kyo. It is the common language we all share. Even at this very moment, someone is chanting Nam-myoho-renge-kyo somewhere on this earth.

In the same way that airwaves are invisible but allow us to connect with what's on TV, when we chant, we can connect with one another heart-to-heart, anytime, anywhere.

I am chanting with all my heart for the growth and happiness of each one of you. Our lives, therefore, are connected by Nam-myoho-renge-kyo. My heart is always together with you.

Today again, please chant in high spirits and advance proudly toward your dreams as true lion cubs.

My greatest dream is for each of you to become great lions and fulfill all your dreams, as you confidently play an active role for the sake of the world.

Lastly, with heartfelt wishes for your growth and victory, I would like to present to you the following poem written by my mentor. He dedicated it to children who were entering the new school year:

> *Let's cheerfully sing*
> *the song of spring,*
> *let's buoyantly dance*
> *the dance of spring.*

With big hearts,
let's grow straight and tall.
Spring, April,
is our time.

—APRIL 2013

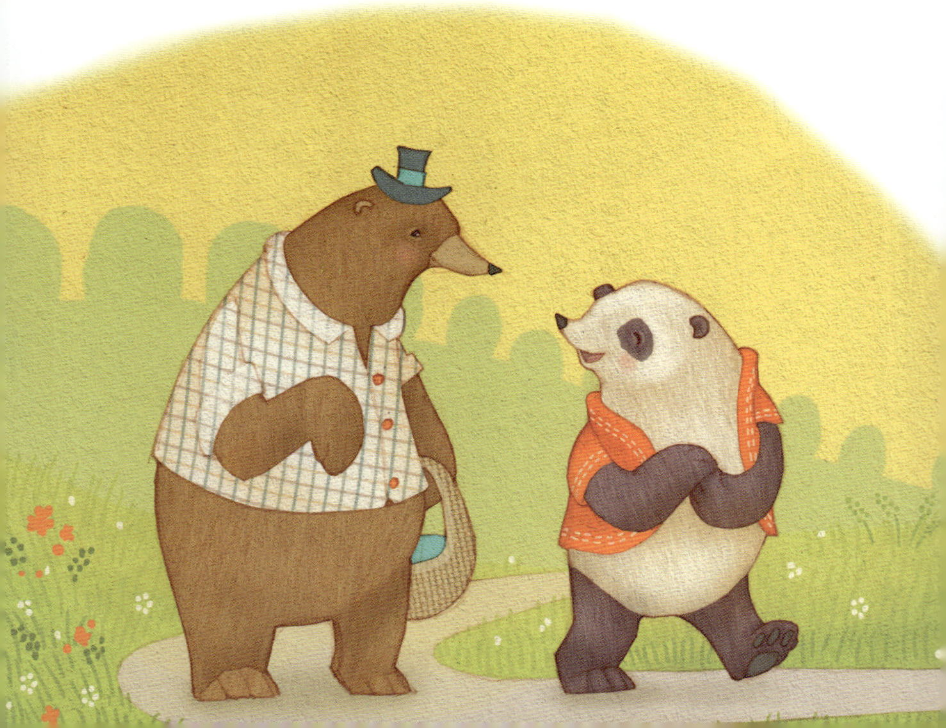

13

Spreading the Spirit of Peace Throughout the World

Today, let us think about what peace means. Have you heard of the great scientist Albert Einstein (1879–1955)? He was also a leader of peace who stood up to rid the world of dangerous nuclear weapons.

Presidents Makiguchi and Toda attended one of the lectures Einstein gave during his visit to Japan (November 1922). Mr. Toda once spoke to us youth of how honored he was to have done so. He also shared with us the great scientist's belief that the most important thing in creating a peaceful world is for us "to change our thinking, to change the heart of [humankind]."[12]

I completely agree. Our hearts can move others' hearts. Our hearts can change others' hearts. Faith in Nichiren Buddhism, more than anything, gives us the strength to do so.

All of your parents and grandparents who are practicing, as well as other SGI members, have been sincerely encouraging others and bringing smiles to their faces. And they continue to do so today.

Where there are smiling faces, hope is created, happiness spreads, and peace shines. Even though you may be going through a sad or difficult time yourself, if you try to encourage someone else, you will feel refreshed. And, of course, the person you encourage will also begin to smile brightly. This is how we SGI members have been encouraging one another, brightening people's hearts, helping people become happy, and spreading the spirit of peace throughout the world.

Such warm circles of support and encouragement have developed into the SGI movement, which has now spread to 192 countries and territories.

An important anniversary in our movement is May 3, Soka Gakkai Day. On a sunny May 3 in 1951, Mr. Toda was inaugurated as the second Soka Gakkai president. At that time, he resolved to rid the world of misery. Carrying on my mentor's spirit, I was inaugurated as the third Soka Gakkai president on May 3, 1960.

May 3 is also known as the "New Year's Day of the SGI." Therefore, it is a day when members set new goals and make fresh resolutions for the year ahead. It's a day they move forward with renewed energy, aiming to achieve kosen-rufu and to do their own human revolution.

I hope that each one of you will also set yourself at least one goal—it doesn't matter what it is—and begin challenging yourself to realize it.

May 3 is also Soka Gakkai Mother's Day. It is a day for thanking and applauding the women's division members, the mothers of kosen-rufu, for their tireless efforts.

In Japan, as in many other countries, we celebrate Mother's Day on the second Sunday of May. But since I thought it would be nice to celebrate twice, I suggested in 1988 that we make May 3 Soka Gakkai Mother's Day. Therefore, on May 3, I ask you to thank your mothers and the local women's division members on my behalf for their constant efforts.

I also made another suggestion in 1988—it was to create a new flag for the women's division. As a result, a wonderful flag was designed. It was a tricolor flag of bright red, yellow, and blue, with a white lily in the middle. Simply waving this flag brightened the scene. It was just like the women themselves.

The SGI flag was then created based on the women's flag.

The red of the flag stands for victory, yellow for glory, and blue for peace. SGI members everywhere have been advancing cheerfully, waving this tricolor flag.

A boys and girls division member in the

Kansai area of Japan was once asked by a friend who saw the tricolor flag, "What country does this flag represent?" He answered proudly, "It's the flag of the SGI, a champion of the people!"

The year 2030—toward which all of you, my young friends, are aiming—will mark the Soka Gakkai's one hundredth anniversary. By that time, many of you will have grown into fine young leaders in your twenties. I am truly looking forward to that time.

The path of kosen-rufu stretches into the eternal future. I hope that when each of you comes to play an active role on the grand stage of the world, the SGI flag will be waving all around the globe as a life-affirming symbol of hope and happiness. And I hope that we will have created a peaceful world where war is outdated.

Our great movement of kosen-rufu has just begun. There is still much work to do. Who is vital to the future of the SGI? It is those who will carry on in our footsteps. In other words, it is all of you! The future of humanity lies within your hearts.

In 1976, I decided to make May 5, which is Children's Day in Japan, Soka Gakkai Successors Day. I did this out of the greatest respect and highest aspirations for each of you. Also, on that occasion, I offered the following six guidelines for the future division:

> *Let's take care of our health.*
> *Let's read books.*
> *Let's always use common sense.*
> *Let's have patience.*
> *Let's make lots of friends.*
> *Let's accumulate good fortune.*

In addition to these six guidelines, I would now like to add the following seventh guideline:

> *Let's cherish our parents.*

Your parents, as SGI members, pray and take action for the happiness of others. They are truly noble and admirable. That's why I would like you to be good sons and daughters.

If you show appreciation to your parents, you can fill their hearts with cheer. Then your parents can encourage others and fill their hearts with cheer as well. And if those people encourage others and this continues, we can eventually brighten the hearts of everyone in the world.

Einstein said that to change people's hearts

"we must begin at home, and with our neighbor."[13] Our great movement of kosen-rufu, which is to build peace and happiness that will last for generations, begins by treasuring our parents.

By being good sons and daughters, you can help advance kosen-rufu one step further. It's not difficult. Nichiren says that simply smiling at your parents two or three times a day is a wonderful way to express your appreciation (see WND-2, 636). Making the effort to study hard is another way. It's your heart that matters.

In May, the leaves on the trees become greener with each passing day. They are growing vigorously as they absorb the sunlight.

You may not notice it yourselves, but each of you is also growing day by day. I can already picture you developing into outstanding young people who will stand tall and proud like "mighty trees of Soka" throughout Japan and the world. Today again, let us set forth together in good cheer, holding high the SGI flag!

—MAY 2013

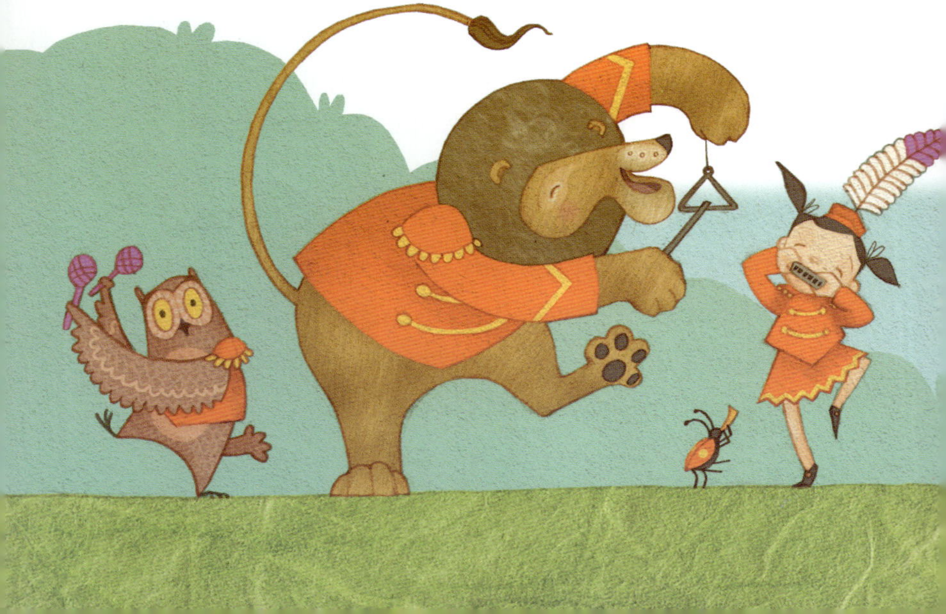

14

The World Is Your Stage!

Today, let's hold our talk and imagine we have a globe or a world map in front of us.

This year again, many bright, lively meetings were held around the world to celebrate May 3, Soka Gakkai Day.

We have SGI members in countries near the equator, where temperatures are high all year round. Members also live in countries near the North and South Poles, where the winters are bitterly cold. Members live in countries with vast prairies, forests, deserts, towering mountains, and mighty rivers. In fact, we now have SGI members in 192 countries and territories. Every day, I am delighted to receive reports of their wonderful activities.

No matter where you go in the world today, there are SGI members who will warmly welcome you as if you were family.

One day, when I was in the fifth grade, my homeroom teacher, Mr. Hiyama, stood in front of a large world map pinned to the classroom wall.

He asked each of us to point to where we wanted to go. When my turn came, I pointed to a wide area in the western part of our neighbor China. It lies in the middle of the Asian continent. I thought that area must be a desert. But Mr. Hiyama explained, "That's Dunhuang in China, a place of many wonderful treasures."

From that time on, I was fascinated by this magical place. Many years later, I became good friends with the Chinese painter Chang Shuhong (1904–94). He was known as the "custodian" of the treasures of Dunhuang.

Eventually, we held an exhibition of some of Dunhuang's colorful wall paintings and other treasures at the Tokyo Fuji Art Museum.

I also chose Dunhuang as the setting for one of the children's books I wrote, titled, *Treasure Castle in the Desert*.[14] It all started from the thoughts and feelings I had as an elementary school student.

I hope that each of you will also take a moment to look at a globe or a map of the world and let your imagination roam. I hope you wonder what different places are like or dream about someday going there.

Reading books allows our minds to travel to wondrous places.

Earlier I mentioned the adventure story *Robinson Crusoe*. It was written about three hundred years ago by a British author named Daniel Defoe (1660–1731). In the novel, a young Englishman named Robinson Crusoe yearns to go to sea and becomes a sailor. During a voyage off the coast of Brazil, however, a storm hits and he is shipwrecked alone on a small desert island. The story goes on to tell how Crusoe starts off his life on this island with only a little food and a few tools.

I remember reading this novel with a world map close at hand. I imagined that I was taking part in the story's adventure. And I asked myself what I would do if I were Crusoe.

My life's mentor, Josei Toda, used this novel as study material for youth. He taught us that no matter how rough life's waves may be, we should face them bravely and live out our lives with courage and wisdom.

My weak physical condition didn't defeat me. I became healthy enough to even travel to the United Kingdom and Brazil, which appear in *Robinson Crusoe.* I made wonderful friends there.

The world is your stage as well. The world map is an invitation to all of you, the main actors of the twenty-first century. The world is calling you.

I hope that you will sometimes spread out a map as you read. Imagine yourself playing an active role in various places in the world, as you continue to develop.

June 6 is Mr. Makiguchi's birthday. He was a great educator and outstanding scholar. He published a book on geography that introduced new ideas and research.

The book, *The Geography of Human Life*, was published in 1903. In it, Mr. Makiguchi pointed out, for example, that the clothes he wore were made of wool that was originally produced in South America or Australia. They were made in England by British people on machines built and powered by coal and iron mined there.

Even just taking a quick look around us, it is clear that our daily lives are inseparably linked to foreign countries. That is why Mr. Makiguchi would express his thanks to people all around the world.

For instance, about 90 percent of the wheat used to make bread in Japan is imported, mostly from the United States, Canada, and Australia. Most of the gasoline for cars and airplanes in Japan is imported. It mainly comes from Middle Eastern countries, such as Saudi Arabia and the United Arab Emirates. And about 80 percent of the lumber used to build houses in Japan comes from Canada and Russia.

In other words, our lives are supported by people throughout the world. Our lives are interconnected. That's why we need to live in peace. This was Mr. Makiguchi's message. He fought against militarism in Japan, as the country ran headlong down the path of war. As a result, he was imprisoned and eventually died in prison for his beliefs.

Mr. Toda carried on his mentor's spirit. He called out: "In the future, we must build a peaceful world of global citizenship. It must be free of national and ethnic division, a world in which everyone can experience true happiness."

Taking these words to heart, SGI members have spread the spirit of friendship and peace throughout the world.

Upon the founding of the SGI [in Guam in 1975], I signed my name in the attendance book. In the column for nationality, I wrote, "World." It expressed my vow as a global citizen to work eternally for the happiness of all people.

I would like to pass on the baton of this mission to each of you, my young friends.

Different world maps are used in different countries. For example, in world maps used in Europe, Japan is usually shown on the far right. People in Japan, however, are used to seeing their country being shown in the middle. In Australia, located in the southern hemisphere, some maps are humorously drawn upside down with the North Pole located on the bottom.

Each country has its own way of looking at the center of the world. And all people are connected to, and their lives are supported by, people around the world. Global citizens are those who realize this and can appreciate others. They can be friends with them, and work for the sake of their happiness.

President Makiguchi, President Toda, and I have lived as global citizens. Those of you who carry on our spirit are sure to become global citizens as well.

Let's spread out our world maps and embark together on a grand journey toward a peaceful future for all!

—JUNE 2013

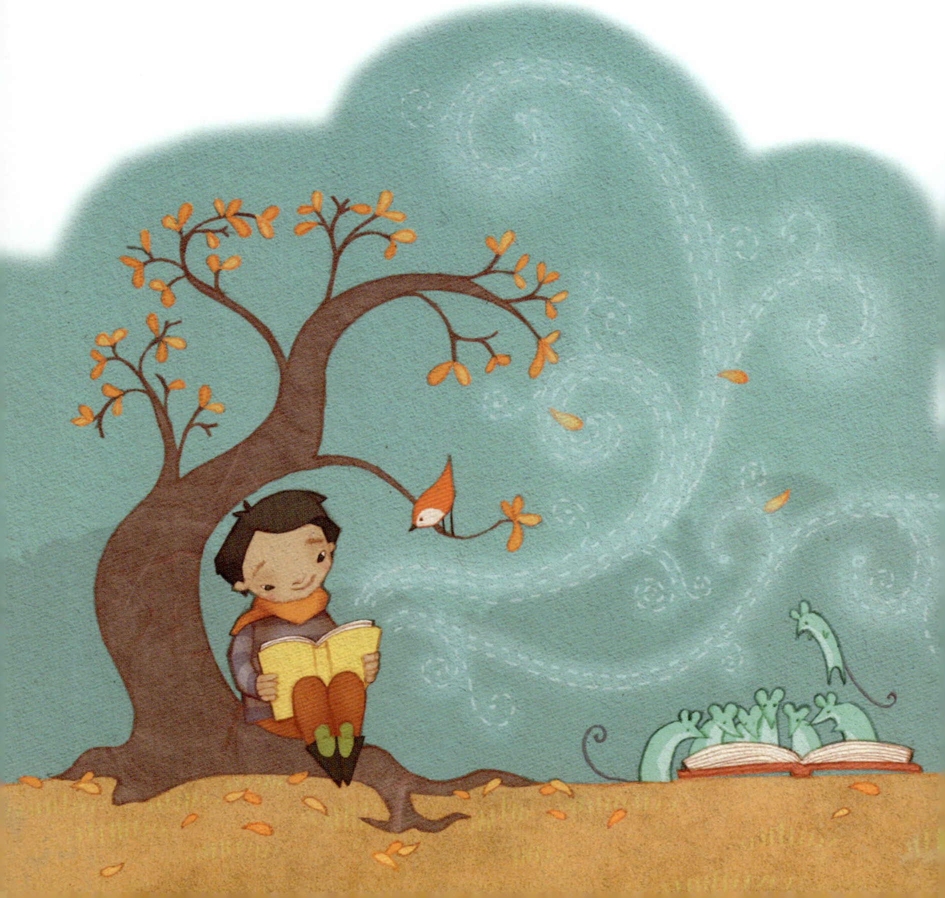

15

Opening Up New Possibilities Through Writing

July marks the midpoint of the year. In a marathon, the midpoint is where the real challenge begins.

In the northern hemisphere it is now summer. In the southern hemisphere it is winter. Both are seasons during which young people can really challenge themselves.

I am writing this today with my prayers for the health and growth of my dear future division members everywhere.

A long time ago in Japan, July was called *fumizuki* or *fuzuki.* That literally means the "month of letters." It is said that this comes from a tradition practiced on July 7, the day of the Star Festival. On that day, people wrote down their wishes on strips of paper and hung them on bamboo branches, like ornaments. This custom continues to this day.

Many people back then wished to become better writers. It seems they wanted to improve their handwriting and composition skills.

How about all of you? When you are given a writing assignment in class or for homework, do you think to yourself: "Oh, no! I don't want to do this," or "I'm not good at writing"? Or perhaps you see a friend who writes well and want to do the same. There's no need to worry, though! We all have the potential to write well.

Nichiren Daishonin says, "Words echo the thoughts of the mind and find expression through the voice" (WND-2, 843). Simply put, when you say what you feel in your heart when you see, hear, and learn something, that becomes your voice. And when you write down what you say, that becomes your writing. The rest is a matter of freely drawing forth that potential you have within you.

When I was in the first grade, I recall my teacher praising me for an essay I wrote. He said, "Well done!" Being praised was a bit embarrassing because it was in front of the entire class.

I didn't quite understand what made my essay stand out from the rest. But I do remember just being totally absorbed in writing what I had seen, thought, and felt.

My classmates were also happy for me saying: "Wow! That's great, Daisaku!" After that, I began to really enjoy writing essays. That experience made me want to write even more.

When I read books, I would copy down phrases or sentences I liked into my notebook. And I would jot down my comments and impressions. I also kept a diary. Such small, steady efforts eventually led to writing longer essays and even novels.

If you find it difficult to write your own sentences, why not start by simply copying down sentences for practice. For instance, what your teacher writes on the blackboard. If you find words or phrases you like as you are reading, you can jot them down in your notebook before you forget. You can even write down lines that touched you when reading a comic book.

The important thing is that you engage in writing. Repeating this process will build your writing skills.

Putting your thoughts into words can also give you a clearer picture of how you actually feel. And curiously enough, as you do so, you'll naturally begin to see what you should write.

Every field of study requires some kind of writing. That's why if you continue studying and growing, your writing ability is sure to improve.

Everyone has some quote or words that have left a lasting impression on them.

Dr. Hideyo Noguchi (1876–1928) was a Japanese doctor from Fukushima Prefecture. He made important contributions throughout the world.[15] During his tough days struggling as a researcher, what encouraged him was a letter from his mother. She had never gone to school. But she practiced the Japanese characters over and over so she could write the letter. It begins like this: "We are all surprised by your success. I, too, am happy for you."

The letter had many spelling and grammar mistakes. But Dr. Noguchi could tell his mother had put her whole heart into writing it. Thinking about this, he read the letter in tears. And thanks to his mother's warm affection, Dr. Noguchi was able to continue his work, saving even more lives.

There's no need to write fancy sentences. What is important is to be able to write from your heart what you truly want to share.

Words that come from the heart will move other people's hearts. They have the power to encourage those who are truly struggling.

As the saying goes: "The pen is mightier than the sword."

Violence and military force may threaten or hurt others. But they cannot inspire positive emotions. Genuine strength lies in the power of the pen, the power of words.

In China, there is the saying: "Writing is a great undertaking that endures for all time."

Courageously written words of justice and truth will live on in future generations.

I truly learned how to write under the training of my mentor, Josei Toda. As a result, no matter what happened I have been able to keep writing energetically to open the way for kosen-rufu, our movement for world peace and human happiness.

At times, I wrote so much that my hand became swollen and I couldn't raise my arm. When I had a fever and was feeling ill, I would keep a tally as I completed each page to help encourage myself to keep writing. I even completed a book this way.

It would not be an overstatement to say that writing has been my life itself.

I have been writing for my fellow members, for the future, and for you, my beloved future division members.

You will all become great leaders of the twenty-first century. I hope that you, too, will use the power of the pen and the power of words to contribute to the worldwide spread of the spirit of Soka. That is, the spirit to treasure life, friendship, justice, courage, and peace.

    To be a good writer, you need to have all six "antennae" up: the six senses of sight, hearing, smell, taste, touch, and emotion.

    Maybe it's a good idea to always keep a notebook handy so you can jot down things that interest you or that you observe in your daily life.

    If you've been assigned a book report, you can write about what fascinated you in the book. You can write about what you learned and what you thought was interesting. Reading can also become a hundred times more fun if you put yourself in the main character's shoes. You can ask yourself what you would do if you were that character and write about that. You can also write your report as if you were recommending the book to a friend, describing specific scenes that were most interesting to you.

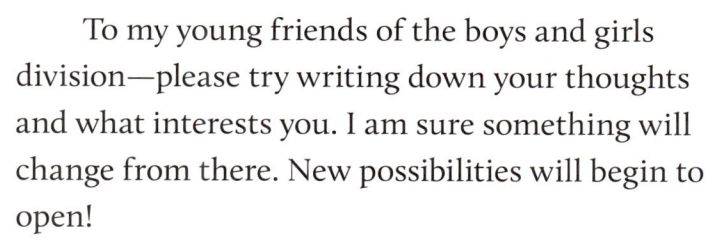

To my young friends of the boys and girls division—please try writing down your thoughts and what interests you. I am sure something will change from there. New possibilities will begin to open!

I regard every piece of writing you have worked hard to compose as a precious treasure. In that spirit, I wish that I could give everyone who challenged themselves to enter this year's essay competition (held in Japan) a "Shin'ichi Yamamoto Prize." Shin'ichi Yamamoto is a pen name I have been using since I was young. You deserve this prize because I believe all of you are fellow writers who write in the same spirit as I do.

To the fathers, mothers, and all those who are helping foster the children: I thank you for your continued support and ask that you please warmly watch over and encourage our precious future division members as they make this summer one of growth and development.

So what shall we write about today? I hope you'll join me this summer in taking on the challenges of writing something new!

—JULY 2013

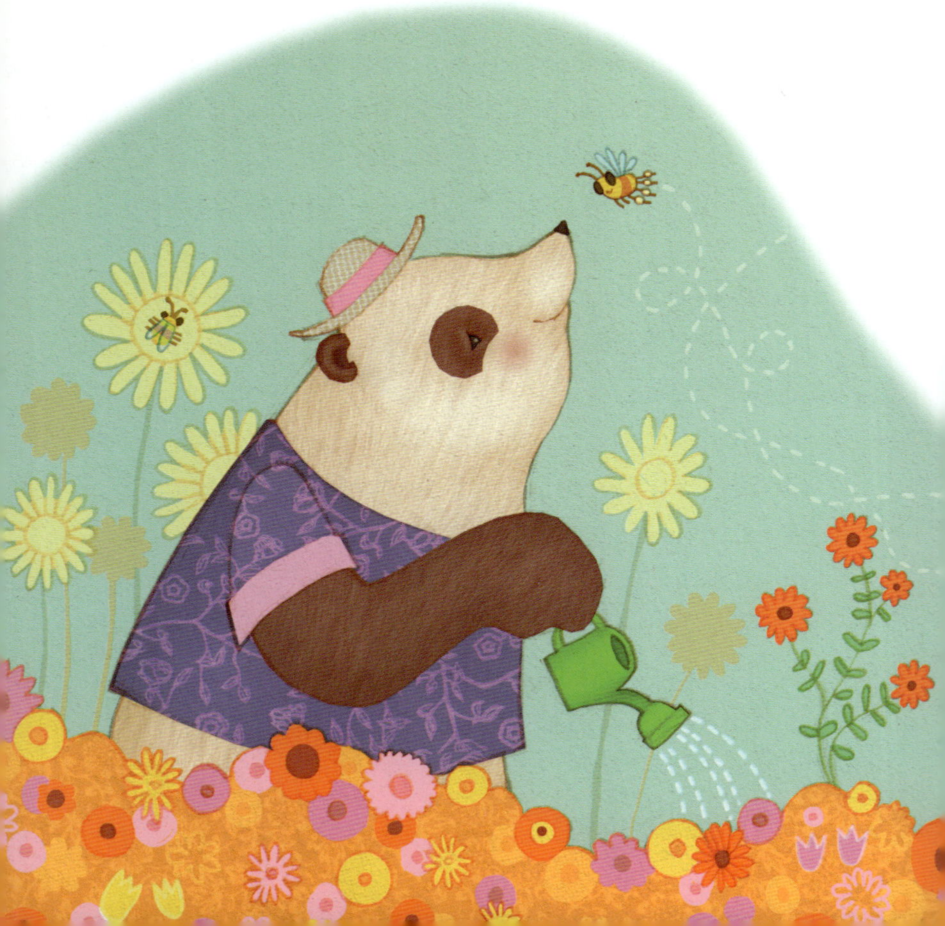

16

Asking Questions Helps Us Grow

Summer flowers, such as morning glories and sunflowers, are now in bloom. Have you ever wondered why many flowers have such beautiful colors?

One reason is that their rich, vivid colors attract bees and butterflies. These help the flowers spread their pollen. One Japanese researcher suggests that another reason for the colors is to protect the flowers from the sun's harmful ultraviolet rays.[16]

Getting enough sun is important. But studies have shown that prolonged exposure to strong ultraviolet rays is harmful, not only for humans but for plants as well. Plants, however, can't wear hats or clothes to protect themselves. They can't move into the shade, like we can. Instead, this researcher says the color in the petals helps protect the flowers.

In a way, then, because flowers make an effort not to be defeated by hardships, they can blossom beautifully. If you think about it this way, the flowers blooming outside are also encouraging us.

Summer is a season of many fun events. I'm sure many of you in Japan are looking forward to attending local fairs, festivals, and fireworks shows.

When I was in elementary school, I could hardly wait for summer vacation. In my hometown of Ota Ward, night fairs would be held near Kamata Station. One night, when I was nine, I went to one of them and walked excitedly around the stalls. They had fishing games, cotton candy, and handcrafted candy sculptures, among other things. At the end of the stalls, there was a tall foreigner selling razors. He'd smile at the passersby and say in broken Japanese, "I love Japan."

But no one was buying the razors. In fact, some were even being mean and teasing him.

At that time, Japan was at war. The battle lines were expanding and many people had started discriminating against foreigners.

I thought: "We're all human. Why are people so mean?"

Once, when my eldest brother returned home on leave from the war, he told me how cruel it was on the battlefield. I myself also experienced terrifying air raids over Tokyo. And I later saw how heartbroken my mother was when we learned that my eldest brother was killed during the war.

"Why do human beings have to hate and hurt each other?" The more I thought about it, the more it didn't make sense. Later, my mentor, Josei Toda, shone a bright ray of light on my heart, which was clouded by this question.

Two years after World War II ended, I met Mr. Toda for the first time at a Soka Gakkai discussion meeting. It was August 14, 1947.

Even though Mr. Toda had been imprisoned for two years during the war, he was never defeated and remained committed to peace and justice.

Mr. Toda said: "I wish to rid the world of all tragedy and misfortune. That is what kosen-rufu is all about. Will you join me?"

I felt I could trust him and decided to join the Soka Gakkai. I made my first step in finding answers to the questions and doubts I had as a young child. And I made my first step in creating a world in which all people could live in peace and happiness as fellow human beings.

Dr. Wangari Maathai (1940–2011) is a renowned Kenyan environmentalist and Nobel Peace Prize winner. She also treasured the spirit of asking "Why?"

When we met (in 2005), she shared with me a story. "One morning, I woke up very early and went outside," she said. "It was still dark; stars were in the sky. Then, suddenly, I saw a shooting star and it scared me. I went back into the house and asked my mother why it was that the sky didn't fall down. My mother said to me: 'The sky won't ever fall, because in the mountains surrounding our farm live giant buffaloes. Those buffaloes have huge horns, and they hold up the sky with them. That's why the sky will never fall.' When she told me that, I didn't feel afraid anymore. I thought that was magical! . . . I remember this story today as a symbol of the wonderful way in which the natural world protects and fosters us."

Through this experience, Dr. Maathai became interested in environmental issues. She continued her studies to become a great scholar in this field. Eventually, she dedicated her life to planting trees throughout Africa to help stop the land from turning into desert.

When I have a dialogue with world leaders such as Dr. Maathai, we ask each other questions. We ask question after question in hopes of learning something new and learning from each other.

Asking questions itself is a step toward new discoveries. It is also a step toward peace, as it helps bring us closer together.

In summer of 2001, I presented a poem to students of an elementary school in the United States.[17] An excerpt of the poem reads:

> *"Why is the sky blue?"*
> *"How does a magnet attract iron?"*
> *"Why did all the dinosaurs die?"*
> *"What is it like at the edges of space?"*

*The mind that questions,
that asks, "Why?" and "How?"—
this is the very heart of science.*

A truly smart person is not someone who simply has a lot of knowledge. A truly smart person is someone who has lots of questions and continues asking "Why?" or "How is that so?" It is someone who keeps thinking hard, even when a quick answer can't be found.

One of my dear friends is former Moscow State University rector and world-renowned physicist Dr. Anatoli Logunov. When Dr. Logunov was young, he heard there was a problem that his math teacher could not solve, even after two days of trying.

He was curious about this problem that would stump even his teacher. He worked on it for many days. Recalling this, he told me happily that when he was finally able to solve the problem, he "felt as if the carnival had come to town."

The more you struggle and the more effort you make, the greater your joy will be when you come to an answer. When you ask "Why?" your brain has to work hard and gives you the chance to grow a lot.

So when you wonder about something, it's important that you ask someone or look up the answer somewhere. Don't just leave it unsolved.

Sometimes, when you pursue one question, you run into another. When that happens, I hope you'll make the effort to ask someone. Or look it up yourself. By repeating this, you'll become smarter and smarter.

There's no need to feel ashamed about not knowing something. To have the spirit to seek answers from others about anything, and to learn about everything—that is the great pride of youth.

Please try out new things and ask many questions, such as, "Why is that?" or "What's this?" Take the time to wonder about things. Such efforts are sure to become the wings of hope that will help you open your world and allow you to embark on new adventures.

—AUGUST 2013

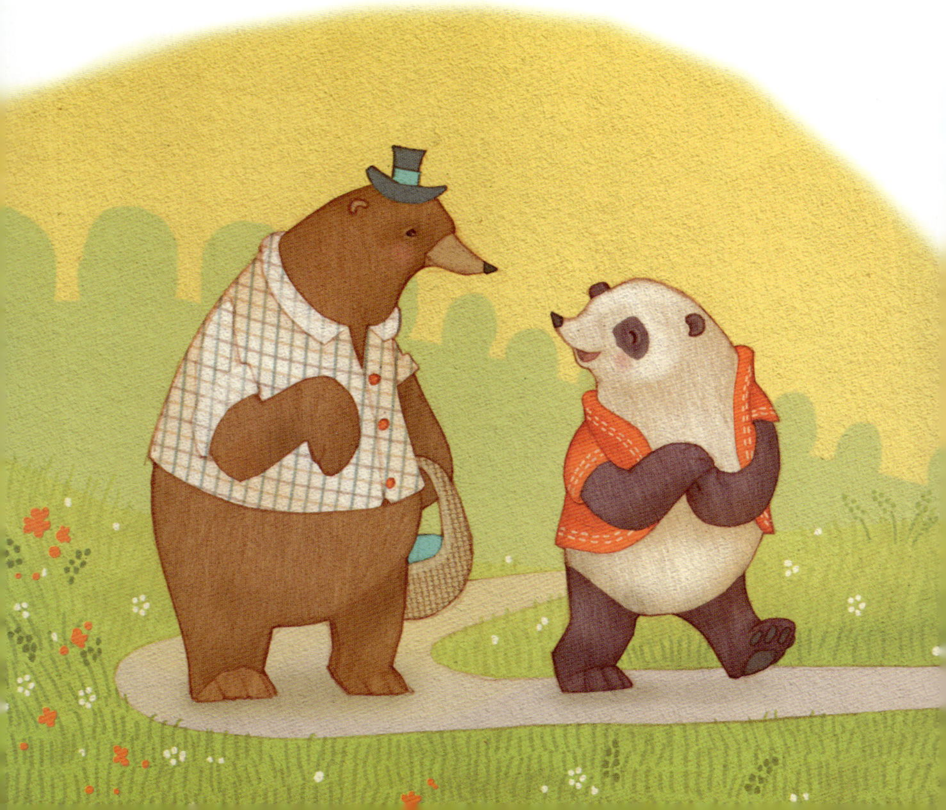

17

Inheriting the "Treasures of Life"

During the summer holidays, I received up-to-date reports on all of your exciting boys and girls division activities from Japan and all around the world. I know that you also did your best in the Soka Family Gatherings held throughout Japan. I was delighted to hear what a fantastic job you did in the starring roles at these events. You led gongyo, acted as emcees, shared experiences, sang songs, and conducted quizzes and games. Thank you all so much!

I would also like to express my earnest thanks to everyone who supported behind the scenes and worked so hard to prepare for these meetings.

Some of you may have attended the Soka Family Gatherings with your grandparents. I am sure they were overjoyed to see you all growing up so cheerfully and energetically. I can really understand how they must feel.

Many of your grandparents have bravely practiced Nichiren Buddhism over many years. They chanted wholeheartedly and worked for the happiness of their friends. But there may have been times when others misunderstood their efforts and criticized them. Even so, they never gave up their faith. No matter how many problems of their own they had, they chanted for their friends who were struggling. They did everything they could to help them. They have given their all alongside me for a better society and for kosen-rufu.

Your parents received the "baton of faith" from your grandparents and now you are taking it up. Those of your grandparents' generation and I could not be happier.

The famous British historian Arnold J. Toynbee believed that the connections between the three generations of a family—grandparents, parents, and children—are very important. He studied the history of the world, and he saw that great social change couldn't take place in a short time. Rather, it would require the efforts of at least three generations to make a difference.[18]

I agree that in organizations and countries alike, the first generation—the founders or pioneers—creates a path where there was none before. The next generation builds a strong foundation. And the third generation works hard to make the organization or country flourish.

In the Soka Gakkai, Presidents Makiguchi and Toda never gave in to any kind of oppression. They devoted their lives to the struggle for peace and justice. And they built a solid foundation for our movement. I inherited their spirit and, as the third president, spread Nichiren Buddhism around the world.

In your families, counting from your grandparents, you are the third generation. If you grow up into outstanding individuals, your family will flourish forever. That will be the greatest victory for your grandparents, who have undergone one trial after another and made such tremendous efforts.

In September in Japan, we have a holiday called Respect for the Aged Day. On this day, we honor the elderly, who have worked long years for their families and society, and celebrate their long lives. It is said that this holiday began in one village in Japan. The mayor there decided to highlight and use the experience and wisdom of the elderly to help the village.

Always remember that nothing is dearer to grandparents than their grandchildren. Your grandfathers and grandmothers are always wishing for your happy and healthy growth. In return, I hope you will show your appreciation by saying a heartfelt "Thank you!" to them. Please spend time with them. Let them see your smiling face or call them on the phone so they can hear your cheerful voice.

People can run or throw more easily when they are young. Our ability to judge what to do when faced with a problem, however, becomes stronger with age.

About thirty thousand years ago, humans started to live long enough so that grandparents and grandchildren could be alive at the same time. The older generation could then share their wisdom and know-how. Since then, humanity has made great advances.

That's why it is such a fortunate thing to be able to hear many stories and learn directly from your grandparents.

Buddhism teaches that respecting the elderly is important for a society to flourish.

In the Soka Gakkai, the group for members over seventy years old is known as the Many Treasures Group. It's named after Many Treasures Buddha.

Many Treasures Buddha appears in the Lotus Sutra to prove to everyone the greatness of the Mystic Law. As his name shows, he is a shining Buddha who has many treasures.

Many Treasures Group members are precious seniors in faith. They have practiced

Nichiren Buddhism with dedication for many years, and they have shown its greatness through their own lives. They possess many treasures, indeed.

What do you think those treasures are? They are the "treasures of life" and "treasures of the heart."

Most of the Many Treasures Group members in Japan lived through World War II and the hard times that followed. They had struggles such as poverty, illness, unhappy families, and problems at work. Along with these, they even took on the problems and sufferings of their friends. They chanted a lot and challenged their circumstances. They gave courage and hope to everyone they met. They assured them that they could definitely overcome their situation and that everybody could become happy without fail.

They may have been much busier than others and had many challenges. But through all those efforts they accumulated mountains of good fortune. We call that "treasures of life" and "treasures of the heart."

If there is someone in a family to carry on the "baton of faith," those treasures will keep on growing and growing. When we chant Nam-myoho-renge-kyo and resolve to do our best, we can inherit all those treasures, all that good fortune. And then through our own efforts, we can gain even more. With such treasures, we will never be defeated, no matter what happens. By turning them into our inner strength, we can cherish big dreams and make them a reality.

I heard a wonderful report from one second grader. Her grandmother had lost an arm in World War II. She learned how her grandmother had dedicated her life to kosen-rufu out of a strong wish for peace. With this important lesson, she resolved to become a person who would work harder for peace than anyone else. I'm sure that when her grandmother heard this, she must have felt as though all her past sufferings were being lifted away.

You were all born in this world thanks to your parents. And your parents were born in this world thanks to your grandparents. When you look at it that way, there has been an endless "relay of life" that has led up to your own birth. If just one of the people in that relay didn't exist, you wouldn't be here today.

Just like each of your families, the human race has been in a long relay of life. It's continued over the past ten thousands, even hundred thousands, and millions of years. And it will go on into the endless future too.

In this precious relay of life, you, my young friends who are now running alongside me, are the honored runners to whom I shall pass the baton in the future.

Because of you, your families, the SGI, and all of humanity will go on forever. You each have an incredibly profound and important mission. With my deepest respect, I will continue to chant for you.

Now, let's make a fresh start with fresh determination!

—SEPTEMBER 2013

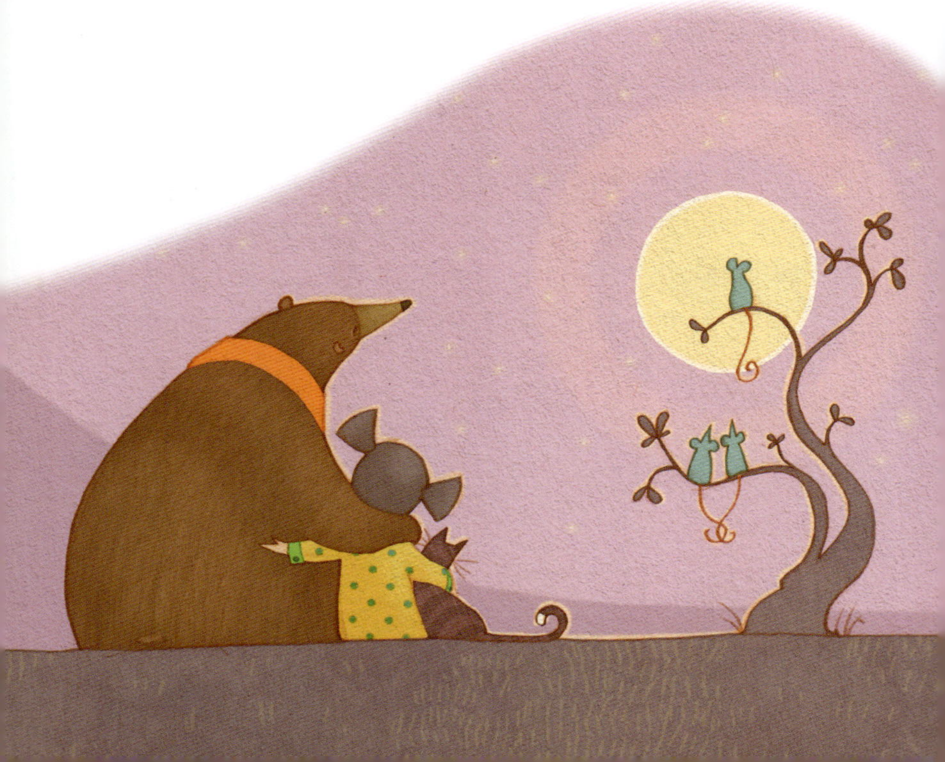

18

Shine as Bright Stars of Hope!

Autumn is a time of clear skies and bright stars.

I'd like to speak with you today as if we were admiring the stars in the night sky together. Or as if we were aboard a spaceship, on an exciting journey through the universe.

Have you ever seen a shooting star? It was summer twenty years ago (August 1993). I remember being in Japan's Gunma Prefecture and seeing a shower of shooting stars together with young friends. It was the Perseid meteor shower. I composed this poem at that time:

> *The cosmos*
> *celebrates us with*
> *this spectacular meteor shower,*
> *scattering jewels of light*
> *like a display of fireworks.*

The universe is endlessly vast. There are all kinds of stars. In the Milky Way galaxy alone, home of our solar system, there are 200 billion stars. Some are brighter than others. The star Rigel in the Orion constellation is extremely bright—about forty thousand times brighter than our sun. But it's so far away that it appears as just a tiny dot in the night sky.

All of those stars are part of our universe. When you think about it that way, the stars in the sky are like friends. They are watching over you and sending warm encouragement.

The star-filled sky is a world of great adventure. You may have heard of constellations such as Leo, Virgo, and Scorpio. Others have more unique names such as Coma Berenices (which means Berenice's Hair), Norma (which means a right angle), and Telescopium (which means "telescope"). Eighty-eight constellations are named in modern astronomy.

Longing to see what lies beyond the night sky, humans succeeded in launching a satellite for the first time on October 4, 1957. This day marked the beginning of the space age. To commemorate it, World Space Week is observed from October 4–10 every year.

Some of you probably know about Japan's *Hayabusa* (Falcon) spacecraft. It went through all kinds of major problems, such as fuel leaks and engine trouble. But for seven years it continued on a miraculous journey of 3.7 billion miles. It was the first spacecraft to bring a piece of an asteroid back to Earth.

The Soka Gakkai's Me and the Universe exhibition features a model of the *Hayabusa* and a moon rock.

In the past twenty years or so, the number of Japanese astronauts has increased, and nearly ten of them have flown into space. In November [2013], Japanese astronaut Koichi Wakata will leave for the International Space Station to live in space for six months and serve as a mission commander [from March–May 2014].

In the future in which all of you will live, I'm sure outer space will feel even closer.

I have met and become friends with a number of astronomers and astronauts. One of them was Aleksandr Serebrov (1944–2013) from Russia. He traveled to space four times and did ten death-defying spacewalks. He first thought about becoming an astronaut one day when, like you, he was still in elementary school.

He was walking home from ice skating practice with his coach, Nikolai. Suddenly, his coach pointed to the night sky. Looking up, he saw what looked like a star speeding through the sky. As he stood back amazed, his coach told him it was an artificial satellite. From that day, he began to gaze up at the night sky regularly and think about this "artificial star" moving through space among countless real stars.

Often a child's sense of wonder becomes a dream, which then serves as a powerful source of energy to advance.

The Soka schools, which I founded, offer a solid education in astronomy. The Kansai Soka schools, in particular, are taking part in EarthKAM. This is the NASA-sponsored educational program that observes Earth with cameras located on the International Space

Station. In other words, this program helps students see our home planet from outer space.

As a matter of fact, we only know what 4 percent of the universe is made up of. There are still many unsolved mysteries about the universe. Your generation has the noble mission to explore these unknown realms. Indeed, your daily studies will enable you to expand your wings of knowledge and set out on an adventure of making fresh discoveries.

I suppose some of you want to become astronauts when you grow up.

Dr. Serebrov emphasized two things that are important for an astronaut. The first is character. In other words, to become an honest, inspiring person. The second is the ability to respect your peers. That means caring for your friends and being able to work with them as a team.

Moreover, he called those who live admirable lives dedicated to helping their fellow human beings "citizens of the universe." Even if they have never ventured into outer space. Our fellow members, including many of your fathers and mothers, dedicate themselves to SGI activities for the sake of others and society. That means they are also model "citizens of the universe."

In the Me and the Universe exhibition, there is a panel titled "We Are Made of Stardust." What exists in our bodies and supports life are elements such as oxygen, hydrogen, carbon. Even gold and silver. These elements actually all came from stars.

Buddhism teaches that our eyes are like the sun and moon. The hair on our head is like the stars. Our veins are like the rivers and streams. Our bones are like rocks and other minerals. Our skin and flesh are like the earth, the hair on our bodies, like the forests, and our breath, like the wind (see WND-2, 848–49). In other words, each human life represents a miniature universe.

Each of you is a unique and special being, the only you in the universe. Buddhism helps you understand how precious you are. It helps you bring forth your infinite potential.

Nam-myoho-renge-kyo is the ultimate rhythm of the universe. The earth keeps rotating and the sun shines down upon us to foster life on our planet. Such activities are carried out in accord with that rhythm. By chanting Nam-myoho-renge-kyo, you can tap the power of the great universe within yourself.

The light of the innumerable stars and the glimmering Milky Way are all right there inside each of you. No matter how hard things may seem, if you chant, you can make your life shine its brightest.

The universe stretches infinitely outward. In the same way, your heart and mind have no limit. There's no end to how much you can grow or how strong you can become.

When difficult or unpleasant things happen, look up at the night sky. In that deep darkness, the stars shine brightly. Compared to the vast universe, your own problems will seem small.

From the perspective of the universe, the Earth is like a single home. There are no boundaries dividing it up. Everyone is a member of the same global family. We should be able to live together in happiness and peace.

In autumn, Venus is visible in the western sky at sunset in Japan. Because it becomes the brightest shortly after sunset, it is also referred to as the Evening Star.

You all have a great mission that only you can accomplish. You have a mission to shine your brightest. You can be a star at reading, or a star at being good to your parents, or a star in sports. It doesn't matter what it is. Just pick one thing in which you can sparkle brilliantly!

My noble young friends with important missions—may you all shine as the brightest stars of hope!

—OCTOBER 2013

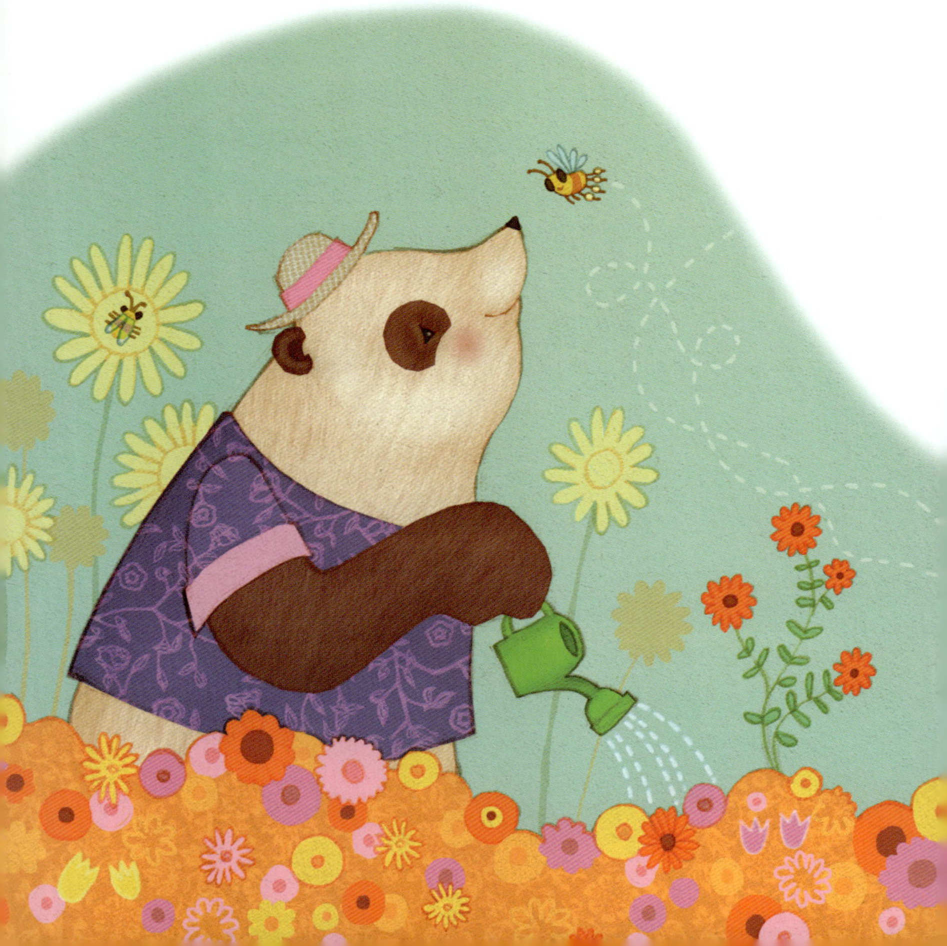

19

Build Great Castles of Happiness and Victory!

It's November, the middle of autumn, soon to be winter. In the cold, northern areas of Japan, it may have already started snowing.

On November 18, we celebrate the day the Soka Gakkai was founded (in 1930). Every year, SGI members, including many of your mothers and fathers, work hard toward this day. It's the birthday of our organization. It will be an especially joyful celebration this year (2013). That's because we've completed the Hall of the Great Vow for Kosen-rufu in Tokyo. Members all around the world have been eagerly waiting for this.

This Hall of the Great Vow is a castle dedicated to you, my most precious young friends. Each of you will carry on the noble mission for the future of kosen-rufu, which aims for world peace and the happiness of all people.

At the time I met my mentor, Josei Toda, the organization had no centers like we have now.

Mr. Toda always used to say, "I feel bad for the members because we don't have our own meeting places."

In response, I said, "Someday, I will build fine centers all over Japan and the world!"

Just as I promised, today we have many centers. Members and friends can gather with joy and cheer and advance filled with hope all across Japan and the world.

I am sure that all of you have also participated in meetings at our centers, along with your parents or your future division leaders.

In Japan, members of behind-the-scenes groups earnestly protect our centers. These include the Gajokai (young men), the Ojokai (men), and the Kojokai (women). The name of each group contains the Chinese character *jo* (meaning "castle" in Japanese). Originally, this was said to mean "a wall built by mounding up earth to protect the people."

Our centers are important castles that exist to support people and help promote kosen-rufu. They are castles that bring happiness to people.

They contribute to the growth and development of our communities and society. Also, after earthquakes and floods, our centers have served as temporary evacuation centers. They've provided shelter for many who were affected.

In addition, some of our centers in different parts of the world are considered historically important buildings.

For example, there's the SGI-UK's Taplow Court Grand Culture Centre, west of London. It was a famous manor house where many important people visited or stayed. These included British prime ministers and the king of Thailand. Even now, it is listed as a building of historical interest.

The SGI-Italy Culture Center, the Villa di Bellagio, is located in Florence. Florence is where Leonardo da Vinci and Michelangelo developed and succeeded as talented artists. Our center there is also considered an important cultural property. The building's history can be traced back almost two thousand years. At that time, it was built as a watchtower along the highway leading to Rome.

And our gathering of the SGI is a castle of peace and happiness for the people. All of you are princes and princesses of this castle of Soka, which extends around the world.

Do you know how large buildings such as castles are built?

The great French writer Romain Rolland (1866–1944) once wrote, "The pyramids were not begun at the top."[19] He's right. A building must be built from its foundation.

The great pyramids of Egypt have stood without falling apart for some forty-five hundred years. That's because they each have a strong foundation.

No matter how good and strong something appears on the outside, if its foundation is weak, it will crumble easily. Everything depends on the foundation.

The foundation of the Hall of the Great Vow for Kosen-rufu also took time and care to build.

The course of your lives is long. But now is the time to build your own foundation. Every problem and worry you have now will help you build a solid, lasting foundation for your life. In that sense, problems serve as the basis on which you can build happiness. No matter how tough things may get, therefore, please overcome your problems and win.

The princes and princesses of the castle of Soka do not give in, no matter what.

The French scientist René Dubos (1901–82) saved many lives through his research in microbiology. I am reminded of a story he told.

One day, hundreds of years ago, three men were hard at work carrying bricks. A passerby asked them, "What are you doing?" One of the men answered, "I am carting bricks." The second answered, "I am working on a wall." And the third answered proudly, "I am building a cathedral."[20]

The same difficult task of carrying heavy bricks has a different meaning depending on the person's heart. If the person believes "I am taking part in the construction of a magnificent building," that person will be able to work filled with pride.

I am sure that all of you sometimes struggle with your daily studies and other activities. But please keep in mind that every effort you make leads to making your dreams come true. Please keep on challenging yourself cheerfully. Believe you are now working on building your own grand castle.

The kind of hopes and ideals you cherish, and the purpose you strive for, will make a big difference in your life.

I sincerely hope that all of you, my young friends, will live with pride and confidence. Please stay true to yourself and have lofty ideals. Never lose sight of your purpose and continue to make efforts to fulfill it. Doing so will allow you to build a brilliant castle of happiness and victory in your heart.

Mr. Toda often shared with us the Soka Gakkai spirit to make our organization a grand castle of capable people.

The Hall of the Great Vow for Kosen-rufu will also shine as a precious castle when each of you develop into capable people and do your best.

That is why the SGI will forever continue to foster capable people. With capable people, we can open the great path of kosen-rufu. We can bring flowers of peace and happiness to bloom. We will be able to advance our movement and achieve victory.

You, boys and girls, are all without a doubt outstanding capable people. More than anything else, I am looking forward to each of you developing your abilities and helping build castles of capable people all around the world.

As always, I am sending you prayers with all my heart. I believe in the growth and victory of each one of you.

Let's make sure to stay healthy and move forward full of energy!

—NOVEMBER 2013

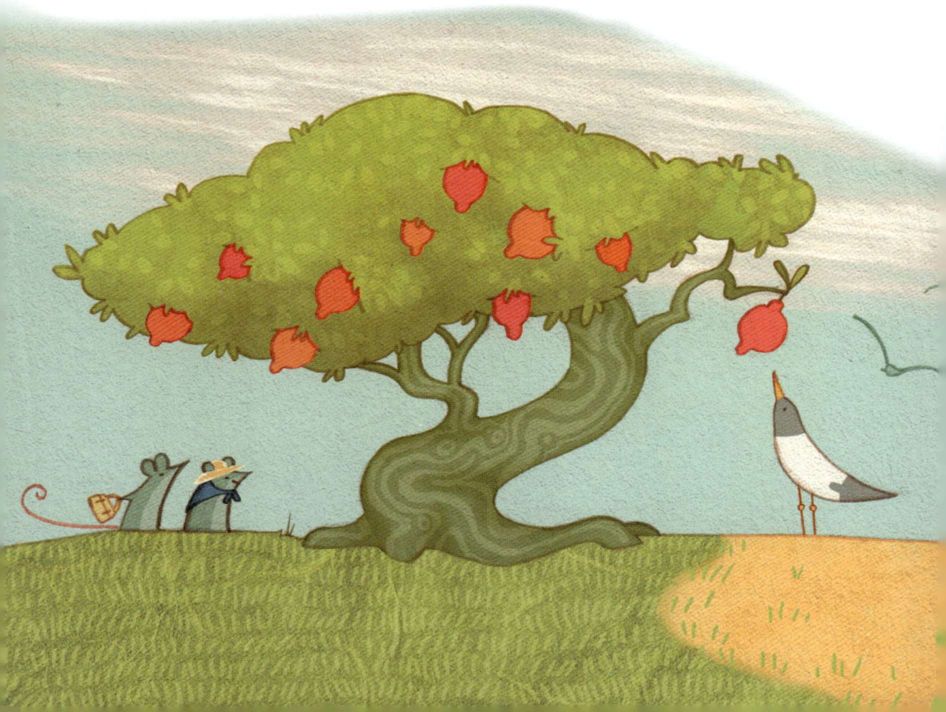

20

Shine as Suns of Peace

Looking back, what kind of year has it been for you? If you were to choose one word, how would you describe it? Perhaps you would choose joyful, cheerful, challenging, or successful. Or maybe it was a year of learning, growth, friendship, or hope? I hope that these are the kinds of words you would choose!

In Japan, we write words using Chinese characters, which have a three-thousand-year history. They are a precious part of humanity's culture and are used by many people around the world. These useful characters, each with its own meaning, were borrowed by Japan from China.

From ancient times, Chinese civilization has greatly influenced Japan's development. Many daily life things in Japan originally came from China. These include rice, tofu, paper and printing techniques, chopsticks, futon mattresses, mirrors, and the Chinese calendar (in which 2014 is the Year of the Horse).

Buddhism, which Shakyamuni taught in India, also traveled through China and the Korean Peninsula before arriving in Japan.

In such ways, Japan owes a great deal to China, Korea, and other neighboring countries of Asia.

Unfortunately, however, war tore apart the connections these countries had for a long time. It caused hurt and suffering to the people of each country.

When I was a child, my father and my eldest brother often told me about their experiences of war. My father was drafted into the army. He was stationed for two years in Seoul, then under Japanese colonial rule. And in World War II, my eldest brother was sent to China as a soldier.

My father and brother were deeply pained by the suffering the war and Japanese occupation inflicted on the people of Asia. They both shared with me that we are all human and such fighting was wrong. Their wish for peace is still deeply engraved in my heart.

Realizing true peace and prosperity in all of Asia was also the heartfelt wish of my mentor, Josei Toda. This was expressed in a poem he composed:

*To the people of Asia
who pray for a glimpse of the moon
through the parting clouds,
let us send, instead,
the light of the sun.*

Mr. Toda continued to pray for the happiness of our friends in Asia, who have suffered war and invasion.

With my mentor's spirit in my heart, I have visited many of our Asian neighbors. I've visited South Korea, China, the Philippines, Malaysia, Singapore, Thailand, Cambodia, Myanmar (Burma), Nepal, India, and Sri Lanka. And I've made efforts to open the path to eternal peace and friendship.

I have also met and spoken with many leaders of Asian countries. These include His Majesty King Bhumibol Adulyadej of Thailand; President K. R. Narayanan (1920–2005) and Prime Minister Rajiv Gandhi (1944–1991) of India; and President Abdurrahman Wahid (1940–2009) of Indonesia. I've also met with many young people who have gone on to become leaders in their societies.

Peace does not exist somewhere far away. It begins with opening our hearts and reaching out in dialogue to one person after another and steadily forging ties of friendship.

In 1968, in front of close to twenty thousand student division members, I proposed that we work to foster friendly relations between Japan and China, whose ties had been cut. Many people in society were against this idea. They criticized me, and some even threatened my life.

But since I am Mr. Toda's disciple, I am not afraid of anything. For the sake of peace in Asia and the world, I courageously continued to take action, staying true to my beliefs.

Four years later, in 1972, Japan and China opened the doors of friendship, and relations between the two countries were restored.

It was in December 1974, in freezing Beijing, that I met with Premier Zhou Enlai (1898–1976), admired as the "father of the Chinese people." He was hospitalized at the time due to a serious illness. But he welcomed me and a small group of Soka Gakkai leaders as trusted friends. I truly felt Premier Zhou's sincere wish to entrust the Soka Gakkai with the future of peace and friendship between the two countries.

The following spring, Soka University welcomed a group of Chinese exchange students. It was the first such group to be admitted to a Japanese university since World War II. They were all excellent students who studied hard.

In October 2013, one of these students spoke at Soka University. She is now a successful translator. During her speech she expressed her wish to join hands with the students of Soka University to further pave the road of friendship between China and Japan. As the university's founder, nothing makes me happier.

Now countries throughout Asia are developing rapidly. They are enjoying more exchanges with the United States, Europe, and countries in other parts of the world. There is no doubt that the twenty-first century is the century in which Asia will shine.

In our dialogue, the great British historian Arnold J. Toynbee expressed his hopes that Japan would cooperate with other Asian countries. He voiced his belief that doing so would help create world peace.[21]

Dr. Toynbee had studied the history of humanity spanning hundreds and thousands of years. He wished for me, someone many years his junior, to spread a wave of dialogue across Asia and the world.

Nichiren says, "It is like the situation when one faces a mirror and makes a bow of obeisance: the image in the mirror likewise makes a bow of obeisance to oneself" (OTT, 165). In other words, those who respect others will be respected by others in return. Countries that respect other countries will be respected by countries throughout the world. They will be able to create peace.

Carrying on the wish shared by my father, eldest brother, and mentor, I have sincerely tried to forge friendly ties with neighboring Asian countries. And from now on, it is your turn to pave the road of peace throughout the world into the twenty-first century. Each of you is a sun of peace and a leading player in building friendships all around the world.

The Chinese character for "light" is said to represent a person carrying a flame overhead. I hope that all of you, my friends of the future division, will carry the flame of courage, of justice, and of friendship in your hearts. I hope you will become people who can impart the light of hope to those around you, shining vibrantly and energetically.

—DECEMBER 2013

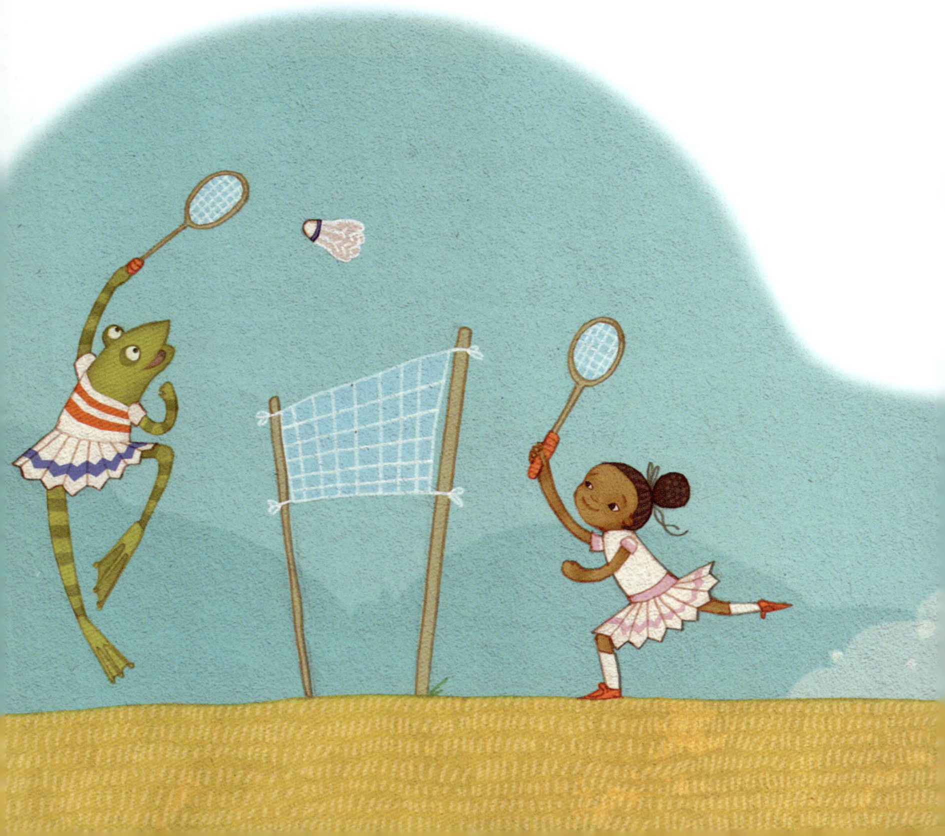

21

Making a Fresh Start Each Day

In 2014, the SGI has begun to further advance with the theme Year of Opening a New Era of Worldwide Kosen-rufu. Our big goal is the Soka Gakkai's one hundredth anniversary in 2030. By that time, many of you will have become leaders playing a central role in our organization. I am looking forward to this more than anything.

At SGI meetings, sometimes members share their determinations toward a new challenge. I'm sure you've heard some of them say that they are going to "achieve their human revolution." You may have thought that human revolution is something hard to understand. But, simply put, *revolution* just means "a big change." So *human revolution* means "making a big change in yourself—a change for the better."

The key to this lies in your heart. In other words, changing from the inside and then powerfully moving forward in the right direction, toward peace and happiness.

Mr. Toda wrote in one of his books, "People can become strong just by changing their attitude." He also wrote: "There's only a slight difference between thinking it's useless to even try and deciding to take on the challenge. If you really give it your all, you'll be able to bring out strength that you always had inside but never used before."

Perhaps you've seen this in your own lives. When you change your attitude, your actions change too. And when your actions change, everything around you changes.

Making a determination unlocks all possibilities.

Human revolution is to keep trying to become a stronger and better person. It is becoming absolutely happy with who you are. It is growing into a person who can fulfill all your wishes and goals.

Your fellow SGI members are working hard every day to do their human revolution. Chanting and doing SGI activities help us do that. Because we make such efforts, the sun always shines in our hearts and we are filled with hope.

The SGI is a group of people dedicated to doing their human revolution.

Actually, human revolution takes place right in our daily lives.

Becoming able to do even one thing you were unable to do before is human revolution. For instance, becoming more physically fit, learning not to lose or forget things, or become willing to do boring chores. If you don't like to study but decide to really make an effort and move forward even a single step, that's also a great example of human revolution.

Things might not go as you wish right away. But if you keep trying, you are definitely changing and in a big way, even though you may not notice it.

Mr. Toda taught me about human revolution. In fact, his book that I quoted from earlier is titled *The Human Revolution.*

At the end of this novel, the main character, modeled after Mr. Toda himself, declares: "My life is now decided!" He pledges to devote himself to kosen-rufu for the sake of world peace and the happiness of all people.

True to these words, after World War II, Mr. Toda expanded the Soka Gakkai from a small group into a large organization. This opened the great path toward building peace and happiness in Japanese society.

As Mr. Toda's disciple, I carried on this noble task. As I mentioned before, I picked up my pen to leave behind a record of my mentor's inspiring life story and spirit.

A genuine disciple follows the mentor's great example. That's why I decided to also name my serialized novel *The Human Revolution.* December 2014 will mark the fiftieth anniversary since I started writing it.

In the course of writing, I sometimes had such a high fever that I needed to cool off my forehead with ice. And when I was too exhausted to even pick up my pen, I dictated my words into a tape recorder. I could continue because I knew readers throughout the world were waiting. I have kept writing because I believe that telling the stories of human revolution will lead to people's victory and happiness.

The *Seikyo Shimbun* now serializes the sequel *The New Human Revolution*. It has just finished publishing the installments chronicling the history of my beloved Tokyo Soka Elementary School.[22]

These two novels describe the stories of human revolution lived out by many members. The great human revolution that began with just Mr. Toda has been carried out by countless others. It is a current that has now grown into a mighty river. Today, dramas of human revolution are unfolding all around the world.

Now, the SGI has spread to 192 countries and territories. The chanting of Nam-myoho-renge-kyo filled with the wish for peace and happiness can be heard somewhere around the world twenty-four hours a day. Mr. Toda's dream has come true.

Just as the sun brightens everything when it rises, your human revolution makes both you and everything around you shine. When you shine, you brighten up your family and your classroom. When your class begins to shine, your whole school begins to shine. And when your school shines, it will foster many capable people who will go out into society to make it a brighter place. In this way, humanity's history as a whole will eventually change for the better.

Human revolution begins when you decide to achieve your goals and chant with that determination.

Just as a new morning dawns each day, you become a new person each day. I hope you will start each new day resolved to do your best. I hope you will kick off the new year with the determination to realize your goals. Let's make this year one of great human revolution!

Opening a new era of worldwide kosen-rufu starts with each of you challenging yourself to do your own human revolution.

—JANUARY 2014

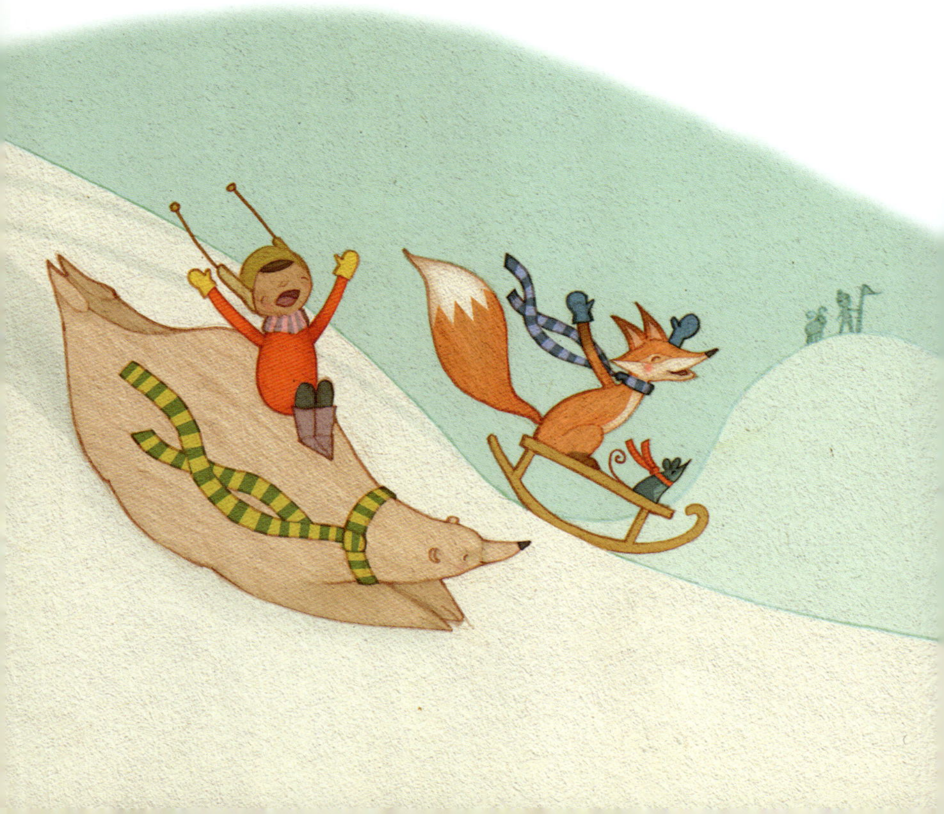

22

Spread Wide the Wings of Your Dreams!

When I was a child, I struggled a lot because my body was weak. So I am chanting every day for you to grow healthy and fit.

Mr. Toda was born in the cold, northern prefecture of Ishikawa. He was raised in Hokkaido, the northernmost part of Japan. He always told us, "Let's strengthen ourselves during the winter!" He also encouraged children: "Winter is not a time to shut yourselves away. It is a time to prepare yourselves for the spring. A time to develop and strengthen your life force in the crisp, refreshing climate."

Please advance with joy and energy each day. Be undefeated by the bitter cold of winter.

In February 2014, the Winter Olympics were held in Sochi, Russia. And in June, the FIFA Soccer World Cup Tournament will begin in Brazil.

In 2020, the Summer Olympics and Paralympics will be held in Tokyo. A new National Stadium will be built near Shinanomachi, where the Soka Gakkai Headquarters is located. It will serve as the main venue for the 2020 Olympics. I am sure that some of our current future division members will participate in these games.

And no doubt some of you are challenging yourselves in your favorite sports, aiming to one day compete against athletes at the international level, including at the Olympics.

Dreams give you hope. They become a source of strength.

The modern-day Olympics also began from the dream to revive the ancient games held in Olympia, Greece.

People's dreams have continued to pave the way toward the future.

Do you know who the first person was to realize the dream of flying into outer space? It was the Soviet cosmonaut Yuri Gagarin (1934–68). He traveled aboard the spacecraft Vostok 1 in 1961. He later famously declared: "The Earth is blue."

Mr. Gagarin visited Japan the following year. At that time, he shared with a group of children that the Earth he saw from outer space looked like a large, soft balloon surrounded by a blue light. He said it was truly a beautiful sight. He spread the dream of traveling in space by sharing his experience.

Mr. Gagarin was in elementary school when chanced to meet an airplane pilot and began to dream about someday becoming one too.

But the road to fulfilling his dream was long and hard. His family was poor. He had to attend night school while he worked during the day. Nonetheless, he continued to study, borrowing books from the library.

Though he faced struggle after struggle, he was filled with joy and excitement. He could feel this way because he never let go of his dream to one day take flight. He told himself that he would definitely fulfill his dream.

Mr. Toda used to say, "Young people should have dreams that seem almost too big to realize." This is because if your dreams are small to begin with, you may end up not being able to accomplish anything meaningful at all.

When you look at where you stand now,

your goal may seem as far as the end of the universe. But please remember that you all have an amazing rocket. This is the rocket of life called "effort." This rocket will help you reach your dream. Everything, including your daily studies at school, will serve as fuel to propel that rocket.

Mr. Gagarin always cherished the words of one of his schoolteachers: "Success favors the bold."[23]

To fulfill your dreams, it's important that you have courage. Have the courage to take that first bold step toward your goal. Say to yourself, "Yes, I'll give it a try!"

Even if you meet unexpected obstacles, the courage to keep trying without giving up or feeling down will open the way to victory.

I, too, had many dreams in my childhood. One of my dreams was to become a journalist because I enjoyed reading books and writing. I also dreamed of someday writing a story that would give others courage and hope.

Also, because I spent my childhood during the dark times of war, I dreamed of planting cherry trees near train stations throughout the land so that when they blossomed, they would brighten people's hearts and lift their spirits.

I was nineteen when I first met Mr. Toda and started practicing Nichiren Buddhism.

Mr. Toda, who had bravely struggled with all his might against those responsible for the war, had a huge dream. It was to rid the world of suffering and misery. It was to bring peace and happiness to everyone. In other words, his dream was to achieve kosen-rufu.

I came to truly admire this amazing dream of his. And, eventually, to realize Mr. Toda's dream became my own dream.

Curiously, while chanting Nam-myoho-renge-kyo and trying hard to make this grand dream of kosen-rufu come true, all of my childhood dreams became a reality as well.

My dream of becoming a journalist came true following the publication of the *Seikyo Shimbun,* the Soka Gakkai's daily newspaper.

My dream of writing a story came true by writing my novels, *The Human Revolution* and *The New Human Revolution.*

And finally, my dream of planting cherry trees came true by planting cherry trees at our community centers and other facilities all throughout Japan and the world.

Your dreams might not come true right away. But with the power of chanting, all your wishes and efforts will definitely bear fruit.

Another big dream that Mr. Toda cherished was to establish a school that exists for the happiness of children. This was a dream that Mr. Toda inherited from his mentor, Mr. Makiguchi. Later, Mr. Toda entrusted this dream to me. He said, "If I cannot achieve this during my lifetime, I'm counting on you, Daisaku."

Determined to realize his dream, I founded the Soka schools, Soka University, Soka Women's College, and Soka University of America. A number of Soka kindergartens have also been established in Japan and throughout the world.

The SGI's network of peace, culture, and education has now spread to 192 countries and territories.

This is all thanks to our members, including many of your grandparents and parents, who have dedicated themselves to realizing Mr. Makiguchi and Mr. Toda's dreams.

I have strived to fulfill the dreams I shared with my mentor. And I have challenged myself in high spirits to this day.

My most cherished dream now is that you, my dear friends of the future division, will try your hardest and make all your dreams come true.

Each of you has a dream that only you can fulfill. You may not have found your dream yet. But if you continue to try hard at each task in front of you, you will surely find something you truly enjoy and wish to pursue. The stage on which you can freely fulfill your mission awaits you.

I believe some of you will become leading figures in your chosen fields. Some of you may become great educators, scientists, or writers. Others may become well-respected politicians or entrepreneurs. Still others may become outstanding athletes or artists. My heart leaps with excitement when I think of this.

Dream big with a big heart! As long as you keep moving forward, there is no limit to what you can dream.

Spread wide the wings of your unique dream and soar into the great skies of hope!

—*FEBRUARY 2014*

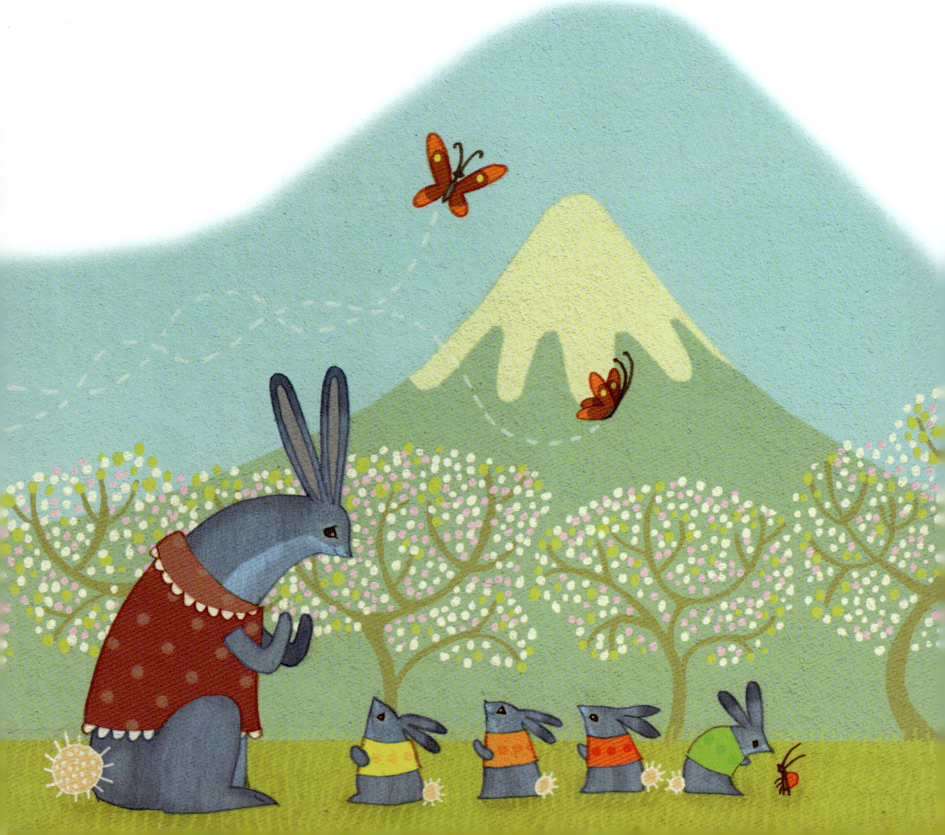

23

Friendship Is a Precious Treasure

As we enter March, with rays of sunshine and flowers beginning to bloom, we feel more and more that spring has arrived. But we should keep in mind that the change from winter to spring can also bring unexpected weather. It may suddenly become cold again or a heavy snow may fall.

Unexpected things may also sometimes happen to you. But I hope you'll see them as chances for great growth and development.

Cherry blossoms have started blooming in Okinawa, the southern part of Japan. Soon those in the more northern regions will follow suit. For Tohoku in the northeast, it will mark the third spring since the March 2011 earthquake and tsunami.

"Light of Happiness Cherry Trees" were planted on the grounds of Soka Gakkai centers throughout the affected areas after the disaster. Their blossoms are sure to bloom beautifully again this year. These trees symbolize the friendship and invincible spirit of the Tohoku members who forge ahead, overcoming any and all hardships together.

Also, Soka University in Tokyo is home to the "Zhou Cherry Tree" and the "Zhou Enlai and Deng Yingchao Cherry Trees." These trees represent and convey to future generations the Soka Gakkai's eternal friendship with the former Chinese premier and his wife.

Friendship is a precious treasure. It is a source of happiness and a starting point for peace.

Nichiren writes, "When a tree has been transplanted, though fierce winds may blow, it will not topple if it has a firm stake to hold it up" (WND-1, 598).

Every big tree starts out as a small sapling. Once it's been planted, the most important thing is that it takes solid root. Unless it puts down deep roots, it will easily be blown down by the slightest gust of wind. That's why you will often see saplings tied to a stake to firmly support them. That way, they can grow into big, mighty trees that can withstand even the fiercest storm.

It is the same thing with people. For instance, you might be studying for an exam or playing a sport. It might get to a point where you think, "Oh, I'm so tired," or "I just want to quit."

But if your friends cheer you on saying: "Don't give in!" "Hang in there!" you will feel inspired to keep going.

With the support of friends, you can accomplish things you might have given up on long ago if you had been alone.

Perhaps some of you have read *Anne of Green Gables*. It's a novel loved by many around the world, written by the Canadian author L. M. Montgomery.

The main character is an orphaned girl named Anne. She is described as having red hair and lots of freckles. People would sometimes make hurtful comments about her. But Anne had an unbeatable spirit. No matter what difficulties she faced, she remained cheerful and strong. She spread wide the wings of her imagination.

Shining with a bright spirit, Anne was always surrounded by smiling friends, wherever she went. Anne treasured every one of these precious people. She says: "There are so many things to be thought over and decided when you're beginning to grow up.... But when I have such good friends... I ought to grow up successfully."[24]

Friends and friendships make life fun and bring more meaning and value to it.

Spring [with the start of the new school year in Japan] is a time when you meet new people, as you go to the next grade and are assigned new homerooms. Some of you must be looking forward to it. Others may be feeling anxious to be in the same class with people you didn't know before. This may be the case especially for those going into middle school.

Let me offer you a helpful tip for making new friends: Be the first to greet and speak to others.

Buddhism started with Shakyamuni Buddha, who was referred to as the "teacher of humanity." He always initiated conversations.

You will definitely be able to make friends so long as you have the courage to talk to others. Keep in mind that they are people just like you, even if it's your first time meeting them. It's also important that you have a big, open heart to talk with others in a spirit of friendship, even though their opinions may differ from yours.

    Sometimes you may disagree with your friends and argue with them. At such times, too, it's important that you take the first step to patch things up and become friends again. As long as you can do this, I'm sure your friendships will deepen. This is what I've always done.

    When you apologize to your friends, please make sure to look them straight in the eye. That way, you can actually turn conflicts into opportunities to become better friends.

    This approach is fine for simple arguments. But it's not the way to deal with bullying, which is a completely different matter. Bullying is a kind of violence that must never be tolerated.

If you are being bullied, there is no reason to be ashamed or embarrassed to talk to someone about it. You shouldn't feel that you're going to worry people by telling them about it. If it's difficult to talk with someone face to face, write a letter. Please remember that many people are there to support you. Keep in mind that your fellow SGI members and I are always on the side of those being bullied.

Even if you are suffering so much that, at times, you feel you'd rather not be alive, I ask that you please cherish your life. It is more precious than anything. Please treasure yourself.

From what I have seen and learned through meeting and speaking with leaders throughout the world, those who have experienced bullying have grown into outstanding individuals. On the other hand, those who bullied others have ended up suffering.

All of you were born having inherited the priceless "baton of life" from your parents, grandparents, and others before them. Please never forget that you have a mission that only you can fulfill.

We are praying for world peace so that we can create societies that value each and every life.

Life means making good friends. But even if you don't now have people you can call genuine friends, there's no need to be impatient. You are sure to make such friends someday.

The future of our movement for kosen-rufu, which is dedicated to realizing world peace and happiness for all people, depends on all of you. My dear friends of the boys and girls division, study hard, chant earnestly, live each day with energy, and build wonderful friendships.

Cherry, plum, peach, and damson blossoms, which bloom in the spring, each have their own beauty. In Buddhism, this principle of "cherry, plum, peach, and damson blossoms" teaches the importance of everyone living true to themselves and shining in their own unique way.

My heart leaps with excitement just thinking about how all of you will have grown into great individuals by the year 2030. At that time, when the Soka Gakkai celebrates its one hundredth anniversary, you will be doing wonderful things in your own special ways.

No matter what trials you may face along the way, please advance with the firm belief that "Winter always turns to spring" (WND-1, 536).

—MARCH 2014

Notes

1. Confucius, *The Analects of Confucius,* trans. Arthur Waley (New York: Vintage Books, 1989), 143.
2. Translated from Japanese. Article in the February 15, 1996, *Seikyo Shimbun*.
3. "Dainanko" (The Great Hero Kusunoki) is the popular name of a song originally titled "Sakurai no ketsubetsu" (Farewell to Sakura). It describes the poignant parting of the brilliant fourteenth-century military tactician Kusunoki Masashige (d. 1336) and his son, Masatsura. As the father departs for battle, his young son declares that he will accompany him, ready to die at his side. But the father asks his son to stay behind and live to carry on his aspirations.
4. James R. Hansen, *First Man: The Life of Neil A. Armstrong* (New York: Simon and Schuster, 2005), 493.
5. Translated from Japanese. Daisaku Ikeda and Ronaldo Mourão, *Tenmongaku to buppo o kataru* (Dialogue on Astronomy and Buddhism) (Tokyo: Daisanbunmei-sha, 2009), 66.
6. Translated from German. Johann Wolfgang von Goethe, *Goethes Gespräche: Gesamtausgabe* (Goethe's Conversations: Complete Compilation), compiled by Woldemar Frhr. von Biedermann and ed. Flodoard Frhr. von Biedermann (Leipzig: F. W. v. Biedermann, 1909), 2:228.

7. See Joseph Rotblat and Daisaku Ikeda, *A Quest for Global Peace: Rotblat and Ikeda on War, Ethics, and the Nuclear Threat* (London: I. B. Tauris & Co. Ltd., 2007), 29–30.
8. Translated from Japanese. From an article in the June 3, 2008, *Seikyo Shimbun*.
9. In the Japanese education system, elementary school consists of six years, and each year, school graduation takes place in March and the new school year begins in April.
10. Eiji Yoshikawa, *Musashi*, trans. Charles S. Terry (Tokyo: Kodansha, 1981), 680.
11. In Japan, the new school year begins in April.
12. William Hermanns, *Einstein and the Poet: In Search of the Cosmic Man* (Brookline, MA: Branden Press, Inc., 1983), 133.
13. Ibid., 55.
14. Not yet available in English.
15. Dr. Hideyo Noguchi was a pioneering bacteriologist known mainly for his research on the cause and prevention of yellow fever.
16. Translated from Japanese. Osamu Tanaka, *Shokubutsu wa sugoi* (Plants Are Amazing) (Tokyo: Chuo Kouron Shinsha, 2012), 139–49.
17. Beyer Elementary School in San Ysidro, California.
18. Translated from Japanese. Arnold J. Toynbee, *Rekishi no kyokun* (Lessons from History) (Tokyo: Iwanami Shoten, 1957), 167.
19. Romain Rolland, *Jean-Christophe*, trans. Gilbert Cannan (New York: Henry Holt and Company, 1913), 54.

20. René Dubos, *The Torch of Life: Continuity in Living Experience* (New York: Pocket Books, Inc., 1963), 151–52.

21. Arnold Toynbee and Daisaku Ikeda, *Choose Life: A Dialogue* (London: I. B. Tauris and Co., Ltd., 2007), 225.

22. See *The New Human Revolution*, volume 27, "Young Shoots."

23. Yuri Gagarin, *Road to the Stars* (Moscow: Foreign Languages Press, n.d.), 83.

24. L. M. Montgomery, *Anne of Green Gables* (New York: Signet Classics, 2003), 251.